My Tailored Journey

How I overcame over 10+ autoimmune issues and found healing and food freedom through Faith

Rebekah Heishman

Tailored Keto Health

About This Book

The Overcomer's Handbook

After overcoming over 10+ autoimmune illnesses, Rebekah is here to chronicle how it all transpired. In this book, she takes you along her miraculous healing journey — challenges and all — and reminds you to be brave and authentically yourself. Her experience, Faith, and wealth of knowledge about health and nutrition have led her to where she is now, helping others along their own journeys while catering to their bioindividual needs.

This book is the overcomer's handbook. It serves as a guide and a helping hand of wisdom along the road to becoming your best self in Christ.

Because you are fearfully and wonderfully made.

"*Your faith has healed you.*"

—Luke 3:48

Foreword

Dr. Ken Berry, M.D.

How many thousands of young people across the world have been mis-diagnosed with an eating disorder? This question may initially seem trivial, but I want you to come back to this question as you read Rebekah's story. With any medical or mental diagnosis, there is some small degree of error. This means a small percentage of people with the diagnosis will be missed, and a few will be given the diagnosis even though they don't have the condition in question. This small degree of error is accepted ultimately because doctors are human, and all make mistakes.

Eating disorders differ from most diagnoses for several reasons. Firstly, there is a definite stigma that comes with such a diagnosis, leaving the patient vulnerable to preconceived notions and unhelpful judgement, both from healthcare providers and their families as well. From the moment of diagnosis, every statement, action, and reaction of the patient is likely to be viewed by both family and doctors through the lens of the disease, leading to the very real danger that either comorbid conditions, or the actual diagnosis itself, will be missed.

Secondly, patients given such a diagnosis are often immersed in a world that is seemingly without an escape hatch. These patients very often lose several degrees of personal freedom by being held in inpatient programs where they are not free to leave. Even in less clinical settings, their behavior is constantly monitored for signs of worrisome or dangerous red flags. Often, family and friends are so consumed in watching for worrisome behavior that there is some loss of support and emotional nourishment needed by the patient. These scenarios often lead the patient to a sort of redefinition of who they are as a person, often replacing the traits that they previously defined themselves with, with the diagnosis in the primary position.

Thirdly, when the therapies and medications used to treat the eating disorder don't correct the condition, there can be a spirit of giving up felt by therapist, family, and especially the patient. Seldom is the diagnosis questioned, or reevaluated, leaving the patient, whose symptoms often worsen, feeling like they are a lost cause and will never be healthy or whole again.

The final and most insidious aspect of the misdiagnosis of an eating disorder is that the real diagnosis is never found. The very food the family has given the patient from their first bite is the root cause and ongoing irritant, but this is almost never considered or experimented with. When the patient explains that certain foods (which everyone else in the family eats!) cause abdominal pain or other symptoms, this is viewed as further evidence of the eating disorder and dutifully reported back to the doctor in charge of the case. Instead of being heard and believed, the patient is ignored. This perfect storm of misdiagnosis, ignoring, and labeling can lead the patient with few options, often making a final solution of self-harm look like their only choice.

I never met Rebekah when she was sick, but I have met with her several times after she was vibrant and well. Imagine how different her story would have been, and how much sooner she could have returned to good health, had her caregivers believed her and helped her experiment with fixing her diet. Her honest and meaningful telling of her story has the potential to help untold numbers of people who have been mis-diagnosed with one of the eating disorders. Her story is one of hope and resilience, and could be the one ray of light penetrating into the currently very dark life of someone in a facility like she describes in this great book.

Ken Berry, M.D.
Holladay, TN

Foreword

Dr. Eric Westman, M.D.

I was surprised to hear of Rebekah's experience as I was reading the book entitled, *The Dietitians Dilemma* by Michelle Hurn. Rebekah was one of the cases of transformation in Michelle's book. I was surprised because the last I had heard of Rebekah was that she was still very sick and living in North Carolina. I was one of many doctors who tried to help Rebekah at that time, but was unsuccessful. I am a specialist that uses dietary treatments, mainly low-carbohydrate diets, in a clinical setting at Duke University. After seeing two of my patients have success with the Atkins Diet around 1998, I started studying and then using a low-carbohydrate diet in a clinical program at Duke. So when I knew Rebekah, I was helping her use a low-carbohydrate, ketogenic diet to treat her multiple medical problems. And as I said, the last I recall, she was still very sick.

As you read her story, Rebekah is no longer sick. She, like many others, had to learn to heal herself. But, you know, in some ways I'm not surprised. When the time is right, whether with or without spiritual guidance, a change in lifestyle and diet can be totally transformative. I see it every day in my clinic. While my approach in a medical clinic does not include direct mention of God or other formal religious guidance, there is clearly some sort of spiritual transformation that occurs. It's almost as if people "wake up". Many addiction programs include a formal acceptance of a higher power. Sugar and processed food addiction is real and may benefit from this approach as well.

In my clinical practice, I'm continually amazed by the profound life-changing experiences that merely a change in food can create. Rebekah's experience of a lifestyle and religious transformation is thrilling to see. I'm confident that her experience will help many others who feel lost and are made ill by the toxic lifestyle that is so common in our society at present.

Congratulations, Rebekah, and thanks for sharing your journey! You are in inspiration!

Eric C. Westman, M.D. MHS
Duke Keto Medicine Clinic
Durham, NC

Contents

Part I

My Story

1

The Inadvertent Check-In

LATE SUMMER, 2017

SO THERE WE SAT: ten or so emaciated, pale young girls and one guy—with our baggy sweater-sleeves and stretchy pant-legs hiked up to soak up every drop of sunshine within our short ten minutes of normalcy and fresh air. I couldn't help but notice that the girls had an impressive amount of leg hair, but we all could not care less.

These outdoor outings were special privileges earned by those who followed all the rules after two weeks of being admitted into the Chapel Hill Eating Disorder Unit (or EDU for short).

We also earned privileges like using the computer for ten minutes each evening, or having lunch with a visitor on the hospital campus.

Other special privileges included getting to leave meal times early to go out into the dayroom—only if we finished within thirty minutes. These were the "Early Birds". Those who couldn't finish before the allotted time had to drink equivalent calories from a gainer shake. I was slower, but never needed to take any of those. I've always enjoyed food.

My battle with malnourishment was not due to caloric restriction in an attempt to achieve any appearance or body composition. I wasn't proud of my protruding hip bones, which made it painful to lie down or sit in a pew at church. I was ashamed of my body and the state I was in. Despite all the consistent hard work I'd put in without avail, I was still suffering in such real ways—increasingly—to a point that I could no longer bear to manage alone or even with the help of multiple functional medicine doctors.

Some kids pushed their food around, others barely took time to chew. We all sat together in this small meal room, but we were all in different places in our own heads.

What an odd thing, I thought to myself, *to bring us all together.* It wasn't really tragic; it was just weird.

My first eye-opening realization in the EDU was that eating disorders are rarely *just that*—there's always more to it. Why do we develop OCD? Where does the desperate need for control come from? There was chaos, distress, and there were red flags long before the fact. I was not the only one with a *special* set of circumstances. Every one of these beautiful people had their own valid reasons. We all made choices that did in fact lead us to this point of danger—some circumstances outside of our own reach, but many still within and improperly handled.

My first dinnertime meal was a burger (my favorite food) between two pieces of bread. I didn't have any sides. I wanted more. I was starving.

Later, I was told that I wasn't allowed to eat as much as the others because my metabolic rate was much too downregulated. My internal organs were shutting down. Their belief was that my stomach was too small, and I did not have the physiological capacity to safely and properly assimilate the amount of food that I wanted to eat. It was a protective protocol on their part.

I never really took the time to consider all the implications of being sub 70 lbs. I *did* appreciate the overall systematic procedures to keep us alive, though... After all, that was the whole point. We were not there to find ease or purpose or even heal from an eating disorder. In the acute ED Unit, we were kept to stay alive.

I WASN'T SUPPOSED TO be here. How could God allow this? On top of everything I was already dealing with, this was the last straw, and I could not handle it. It wasn't fair! (But life isn't about being fair).

Only a short time prior to this, I was diagnosed with Chronic Lyme Disease (*2017, age 24 I was deemed medically unstable to work, disabled*). I couldn't afford the expensive supplements, IV therapies, hyperbaric chamber sessions, and ozone treatments that were recommended and apparently necessary if I hoped to live a somewhat "normal" life.

Spending thousands of dollars hooked up to an IV on a weekly basis is *not* normal. What's more is that it's neither affordable, nor sustainable. With as much pain and fear that I felt and based my decisions on, I still had peace walking away from those doctors.

I continued to work with functional medicine doctors who really didn't have many answers beyond what I was already doing or had already tried. Low Carb, Low FODmaps, Paleo, AIP (Autoimmune Protocol), Whole 30, strict keto, all the supplements, acupuncture, dry needle, massage. I even tried ozone therapy as well as Platelet-rich plasma (PRP) therapy as a huge blessing from a relative. These things did not make any significant change or impact in my healing journey. I continued to worsen and suffer. I now see that I was not supported at a systemic level in order to receive the benefits of these therapies.

I started to feel as if I was running in circles. It was so unsettling. I didn't struggle with patience in the process—I just wanted to find the right track to begin with.

So finally, my Functional Medicine Doctor (or FMD) said that she wanted me to go to the multi specialist unit at the University of North Carolina (UNC) at Chapel Hill. She said she was going to make a phone call to one of the doctors there. I still, to this day, do not know who I was supposed to have seen.

My mom drove me to the emergency room, which is where my FMD had told me to check in. She told me that once I was in, they would connect me with the right person. I look back now on the absurdity of this idea, but I did what I was told.

Mom dropped me off at the front door and planned to meet me back inside in the main waiting room. I explained at the front desk that I was sent by my FMD.

"ARE YOU HAVING ANY thoughts of harming yourself?" asked the man at the front desk of the ER.

"Well, yes and no... I have autoimmune disease, so essentially my body is attacking itself," I answered.

As much as I desperately tried to keep things lighthearted, especially during tough times, I had *really done it this time.*

This was the *wrong* time and place to use a playful choice of words.

That singular question about harming myself was not meant as a kind gesture—it was a careful procedure meant to separate those who are a danger to themselves from those who aren't. In a moment of trying to humor myself, I complicated something that could have been nothing. *I could have left within a few hours.* But God already knew what was about to unfold. Perhaps I really was a danger to myself. Perhaps my humor still held a truth that I wasn't ready to receive or admit to... I had really done it this time.

I was sent straight to the psych ward, which was in the basement level of the hospital. They asked me to wait in a room the size of a kitchen pantry. It was windowless except for one small square slit in the door. I later learned this was the trauma unit.

They locked the door upon leaving. My mom was nowhere to be seen.

I remember actually imagining shooting my own two feet and how that would have been more convenient than this. I was already an anxious mess 99.9% of the time. What are the chances of someone *accidentally* admitting themselves into a psych ward? You tell me.

After simmering down a bit, I focused my attention on two younger teenage girls in the room beyond the locked door. I could see them through a window—the only opening to the world outside this dark room I was in. They were wearing hospital gowns, had really short hair, and looked absolutely exhausted. They were sitting on the floor making what looked like very awkward conversation. I felt uncomfortable for them. I also wanted to tell them it was all going to be okay. That's what I kept telling myself. They didn't seem stable or like they should be alone. *Nobody is helping them. They need more than just a protected room to sit in. They need encouragement, nourishment, to be heard, and to be loved.*

This thought process was a trend. Whatever my heart needed to believe for myself, I would look for opportunities to speak that truth over others and their own circumstances if it did or could apply. It was much easier to believe for others than for myself. It always seemed that way.

FINALLY, MOM SHOWED UP. She was led into the room and now we both were locked in this tiny, unlit, and unwelcoming space with no idea what was next or how long we would be waiting. I wasn't allowed to leave.

"This is ridiculous," she said. "Why do they think you need to be held in a rubber room?"

I explained that I probably could have used a better choice of words concerning my having thoughts of harming myself or being a danger to myself. After another hour of waiting, I was led to the regular Urgent Care floor. Basic labs were getting started, and at least I was getting somewhere.

My mom never complained about the wait. She stayed with me. She wanted this to all be over. She wanted answers as much as I did. Our relationship had become so strained lately, but she never loved me less when I became more difficult to be around.

I was severely dehydrated. My blood sugar was "low", but I assured them it was all right and that I was on a ketogenic diet. They were extremely fussy, but finally backed off after I called them out multiple times about trying to hook me up to an IV with glucose. I would willingly put up a fight to avoid intravenous glucose. After over fifteen years of Keto, and Paleo before that, I knew that sugar made me unwell mentally and physically. I knew it triggered cystic acne, mood disorders, inflammation, chronic pain, and even emotional instability.

> ***A low blood sugar within traditional medicine is anything below 70mg/dl. For a fat adapted individual, a low blood sugar is not dangerous like it is for someone who relies on glucose for fuel.***[1]

You'd think that an emergency room would move at a quicker pace. My mom and I really wanted to locate the doctor I was sent to see, so we decided to wait it out (and we didn't really feel like there was much of a choice as I was seemingly unstable).

LATER ON, MY MOM went out to get food. I asked her to bring back my typical dinner of raw grass-fed beef, drenched in olive oil with a side of salted avocado. I used to add cayenne pepper, black pepper, cinnamon, and sometimes cumin and fresh thyme to the beef. It was really quite delicious. Looking back, I now see that I was loading up on histamine, seed oil, and oxalates. Thank goodness I was getting the beef part right.

As you can imagine, the nurses were not very excited about my meal. I explained how the ketogenic diet had been the only thing that had made a difference thus far and was, for the most part, why I wasn't still bedbound. Being in ketosis mitigated so many of the symptoms that kept me down. It alleviated non-epileptic seizures, severe fatigue, and much of the fibromyalgia and connective tissue disease inflammation and discomfort.

We were ignored the entire night. I walked laps around the tiny space. I remember using the phone at least 10 times before turning in for the night. They still had my cell phone confiscated. My FMD wasn't answering. *Where was this specialist? Had she forgotten to call him?*

I never slept that night. I tried to get comfortable, cramming deflated scratchy pillows under the boney crevices of my body. I lay awake, distracted by red blinking lights and the not-so-distant sounds of beeping and snoring.

The next day was pretty much the same. I was getting discouraged, impatient, and irritated.

Then, things got weird.

AFTER ANOTHER ROUND OF failed attempts to reach my doctor, I found my mom on the other side of a circular room. She was sitting on a bench next to an area with children's books and puzzles. She looked extremely upset and somewhat distant.

She wouldn't say anything at first. After a couple of minutes, she cracked and explained something that made my stomach turn sour in a matter of seconds.

"The nurse explained to me that your stomach is too small, and you might never recover. You need to be hooked up to a feeding tube."

What!? I couldn't believe the nerve of this nurse. I knew she didn't like that I was eating a ketogenic diet, but did she really have to sneak around talking to my mom behind my back, telling her things to scare her into compliance?

I felt defensive over my mom, as she was alarmed and so distraught. I was eating half a pound of ground beef and entire avocados. I was pretty sure the size of my stomach was not the issue.

After that, they said they were moving me to another level until I could see my specialist doctor. They led me to believe that I was still headed in the right direction.

Where I actually ended up was the crisis unit.

THIS PLACE, THE CRISIS unit, was actually pretty cool. I was sad when I found out my mom couldn't come along. I would have given her the biggest hug if I had known that I wouldn't be seeing her for another month and a half, and that our relationship would be torn and severed for so long afterwards.

The woman in charge of the crisis unit was an instant friend. She was a stocky, down-to-earth woman. She could tell I was being manipulated, and that I had a sense I was being mistreated. She gave me a bit of extra privacy and grace that the other girls did not receive. The unit was pretty laid-back. We all had our own separate bedrooms, and we met for mealtimes and an optional yoga time in the evening.

I still had a cooler bag full of raw ground beef and avocados to eat, so I turned down the option to order from the extensive menu, all options from restaurants in the area. Mexican, steakhouses, Chinese, Italian.

Apparently, all of this was covered by health insurance. Meal time looked like a cruise line buffet for each person. It was legit!

SEVEN OR SO YOUNG women sat around the big table talking about...well, our crises.

Two were pregnant, and all were dealing with substance abuse. I didn't feel uncomfortable, but I still didn't feel like I was in the right place.

I continued to call my doctor whenever I had the chance.

I unloaded my things into the dresser drawers, only to pack them right back up before the sun set, when I was redirected and transferred to my final destination at UNC: The UNC Eating Disorder Unit.

---

1. Hypoglycemia: https://www.mayoclinic.org/diseases-conditions/hypoglycemia/symptoms-causes/syc-20373685

2

Life In the EDU

SO NOW WE UNDERSTAND *how* I had gotten to the eating disorder unit. The entire process took two whole days, and I was in limbo waiting until I was finally brought in to the EDU. Through circumstances nobody would have guessed, I found myself in the *last* place I felt I needed to be. I *thought* my family, friends, and doctors would have agreed... I thought.

"Hey! I know that this probably feels crazy to you right now. I just wanted to introduce myself. We're going to be roommates. I'm Katie."

She looked like a mermaid. She had the most beautiful, long, blonde hair I'd ever seen. It was unkempt but still beautiful. She was wearing what looked like a comfortable hoodie and had glasses. She instantly seemed like somebody I would converse with in the outside world.

Why is she so happy? I thought to myself. She seemed so comfortable and confident. *Definitely the pack leader*, I decided.

I was extremely disoriented and exhausted. This felt similar to what I felt when moving seven states away from my childhood hometown in the 6th grade. I left everyone I knew and loved—everything that *knew and loved me*... I didn't want to get to know anyone. I wasn't supposed to be here. I felt betrayed by the nurse and doctors who conspired to force this whole situation. I felt invisible and misunderstood—and though those feelings were not unfamiliar, this was the biggest letdown yet. This was the moment I would have expected someone to stand up for me—someone from all the people I thought were on my team still rooting for me. I felt as if it was all a lie. I doubted every single relationship in my life, including my relationship with Christ.

There were five or so other kids in this common area—clearly much younger than Katie and I. They were all watching me—observing me; I could not care less. I couldn't get over the fact that I was here. All the misdiagnoses, accusations, and distrust weighed heavily on me, like a dark angel looking down on me and laughing. I felt shame and embarrassment. Where had all my efforts got me? Nowhere. I had knowledge, but lacked wisdom and discernment. I had Faith, but lived from fear.

I was anchored at the front desk with all my things, determined not to settle or relent. "I don't have an eating disorder. I have severe autoimmune issues. I'm not supposed to be here. I need those supplements. I can't eat hospital food." On and on I went with all my facts and reasonings. They didn't even pretend to care. It's almost like they had recited this very conversation at least a hundred times with others before me. I felt insignificant, tiny, invisible. Probably for the first time in my life, I felt a small sample of just how weak I really was. I saw myself from a new perspective. I was at the mercy of those who didn't believe anything I said. I depended on them for my life. I had no voice or input that would be considered. I was fighting, but there wasn't even a match. I was just flailing—wasting energy, self-defeating, tiring myself out.

I knew that everything I was saying was making my case worse, but I couldn't *not* share my truth. It was second nature. I was being humbled at this time—not even enough to consciously acknowledge, but it was starting to happen. I was breaking down. Inside, I was trembling. I was getting ready to submit to something that I simply could not control—and that was terrifying.

The bedroom was set up with two parallel desks and twin beds, with a giant window in between. The window almost covered the entire wall, which is the first thing you noticed when you opened the door to the room. The desks and beds were right alongside either wall. You could see a bit of the campus outside the room. We had a great view of the sunrise each morning. Katie's bed looked comfortable and inviting, with a giant body pillow and a home-made tie off fleece blanket. Her desk was inhabited by books and heartfelt letters, cards, and drawings.

She seemed to have an obsession with oversized t-shirts, and I admired her oversized sweatshirts. I knew that none of this was new to her.

Our bathroom was kept locked. A nurse had to monitor us while we used the restroom. We had to measure and report our urine and defecation (all of it). For the next month, everything in and everything out was closely monitored—which didn't seem like a helpful way to overcome any type of eating disorder. The mirror was nothing but a reflection of light. It was so blurry that I could just barely make out the shadow of my face. Now I understood the unibrows and overall "unkempt" trend in this unit. It wasn't so much that these kids were lacking motivation—which had been my initial thought. It was that we had our senses literally jipped and jinxed.

I won't lie—I was immediately excited about this. I *love* oversized sweaters, fuzzy socks, slippers, and not spending time on my hair. I do think it's important to have stretchy, and even some baggy, clothing when trying to gain weight. It's part of having a healthy goal and making it real. I used a pair of bell-bottomed yoga pants to scale my gains. By the time I left, they were almost fitting. I remember laying in bed every night, taking note of whether or not my thigh gap had closed yet, and imagining what it would feel like when it did. I often imagined having more warmth and cushion on my frail, cold, bony body.

EACH MORNING WE HAD a weigh-in after using the restroom. We had to face backwards so we couldn't read the scale (because that could be a trigger). If we ever had low blood sugar, we weren't supposed to inquire about it. We just had to drink the apple juice or take the glucose tablet—even if it made me feel worse, even to the point of vomiting. I was hypoglycemic, and the sugar was making me crash harder. I use the word "crash" in a literal sense. When sugar is quickly elevated, insulin kicks in sometimes more than what is necessarily helpful. Insulin helps to regulate and stabilize glucose—blood sugar levels. When we have insulin resistance, this mechanism fails and causes all sorts of chaos. Insulin resistance can manifest as elevated blood sugars, but it can also result in hypoglycemia—low blood sugars—that only get lower with more sugar. I've been prediabetic, and at one point I was almost diagnosed with delayed onset type 1 diabetes. What I knew beyond a shadow of a doubt: sugar made everything *way* worse. Not only did it set me off on a blood sugar rollercoaster, but it caused inflammation and autoimmune flareups. It exacerbated and perpetuated mood disorders.

> ***Hypoglycemia*** *(also known as low blood glucose, low blood sugar) is a condition resulting when the blood glucose levels drop below the specified limits (4 mmol/L or 72mg/dL). It causes irregular or rapid heartbeat, pale skin, numbness of lips, tongue or cheek, and sweating.*
>
> *Symptoms are sudden and range from mild to severe:*
>
> *Excessive sweating*
> *Tiredness, lightheadedness*
> *Feeling dizzy and weak*
> *Being pale*
> *A sudden feeling of excess hunger*
> *Increased heart rate*
> *Blurred vision*
> *Confusion*
> *Irritable or nervous*
> *Symptoms of hypoglycemia during sleep include:*
> *Having nightmares*
> *Crying in sleep*
> *Excessive sweating so as to dampen your clothes*
> *Feeling tired, irritated, or confused after waking up*
>
> *Severe cases can lead to:*

Convulsions/seizures
Delirium
Fainting
Loss of consciousness[1]

The moment they allowed me to pair peanut butter (fat and protein) with an apple, my blood sugars started to stabilize. Instead of riding the Drop Tower, I was on a kiddie coaster. They didn't like added fat or protein beyond the macro and caloric plan for that phase or day.

Everything was recorded. Every *sip* of water, recorded. Mustard packets were regulated, tightly. I was rewarded for eating quicker than what was comfortable, but I did it because I knew we were being timed. I was told that gluten intolerance was all in my head. I was being brainwashed and challenged for every belief I had around food, nutrition, and fueling my body. Yet, I felt less connected or trusting of my own body with each passing hour in this place. All my joint and body aches quickly returned worse than they had been for months. I made sure that wasn't just all in my head. I tried to have a good attitude. I was in so much pain.

"We are about to meet with the dietitian." One of the nurses tipped me off as I left the dining room on that first day.

The dietician, Leah, visited every weekday for about 45 minutes to sit down with everyone while we filled out our meal plans for the next day. She was a very healthy-looking young lady, only a bit older than my roommate and I. She also had beautiful, long, silky hair, but hers was dark. Her boyfriend would sometimes come in with her. I admired what I imagined her life to be. I admired some of the nurses here, too. One particular nurse always raved about my essential oils. They allowed me to keep these and Tiger Balm in my "sharps" bin. This was a bin containing items not allowed in the bedroom, like tweezers and razors. These were only accessible under supervision. I used my essential oils on my pillowcase and on my sweatshirt. This particular nurse seemed like someone who listened to The Cure and shopped at Whole Foods.

At home, my mom would ask me to cover my door if I diffused certain oils. It felt good to be appreciated for them. Something so little really lifted my spirits a lot. More of the painful and empty spaces of my heart were being exposed. I was lonely, and I had been for a while now. Health issues just took over one day to the point of no—easy—return...

I saw this nurse in front of our building on a skateboard, weaving around a friend and laughing. It was so nice to be reminded that I wasn't stuck here forever. My favorite season (Fall) was arriving out in the real world.

These nurses had lives and families to go back to after all this madness. But for us, it felt never-ending. For many of these kids, it was almost a lifetime of chaos, numbness, misunderstandings, pain, internal conflict, digestive issues, weakness, fear, anxiety, shame, and addiction.

THE FIRST TIME LEAH passed out our meal sheets and I glanced down at the different options, I became more stressed out with each passing tensed breath. I was about to be eating *a lot* of carbohydrates, more than I ever had. My pancreas had been happily chillaxing with a low-carb, ketogenic diet for the past 15 years.

> ***The pancreas is responsible for producing insulin. When one eats a low-carb diet, the amount of insulin needed becomes less. This often results in impaired insulin sensitivity. Insulin resistance can occur when the pancreas is being asked to work overtime—for foods that have a high glycemic effect, such as sugar and carbs.***[2]

The following month, I ate more processed food, seed oils, sugar, and gluten than I had ever fathomed eating. I had only ever had nightmares about accidentally consuming even a fraction of the amount of the types of foods I ate here. I won't lie—a small part of me was psyched to be forced to do something so extreme. I didn't have a choice, so I may as well try to enjoy it, right? I love apples. Unfortunately, I got a lot of the dark red, grainy ones. But there were some pink ladies and honeycrisp that were pretty fantastic. I had them dipped in Greek yogurt, and sometimes peanut butter too. I was proud of myself for making the most of my options.

Our allotted moderate protein was a saving grace—alongside tiny amounts of fat. These fats were only to be found in margarine, peanut butter, and cheese.

That first day, I noticed Katie filled out her meal sheet as if it was a test she had memorized every answer to beforehand. Heck, she could have written it herself. I didn't even pick up my pencil. The only options I felt comfortable with were scrambled eggs with a side of salsa, and the salmon dinner.

I waited until the others were finished and asked to speak with Leah privately. We stepped into the only private sitting room in the whole unit.

It had two couches, a small wall-mounted TV, and a circular dining table. All four walls had windows. Everyone in the main area could look in from outside and even read our lips if they wanted.

Before we even sat down to talk, I was told I needed to have my afternoon snack before dinnertime.

My first snack in the eating disorder unit was a packet of saltine crackers and an orange.

I ate them while explaining that I *did not* tolerate sugar or carbohydrates. I explained I did not have an eating disorder and that I was fighting serious disease and autoimmune disorders. She listened, but couldn't help. She recommended I try to choose the lower carb options I felt comfortable with for starters. I appreciated her willingness to listen, but no rules would be bent for me.

I was ready for bed (to escape from reality). I wanted so badly to fall into a deep sleep and to wake up in my own bedroom back home.

Suddenly, the misunderstandings and arguments with my parents seemed less problematic. But somehow still, it felt nice to be heard by Leah, or appreciated for my essential oils. The last half year or so had been so hard at home. I was a burden to myself and everyone around me. I was a disappointment, a stressor, a cause for concern. It seemed like when I tried to lighten things up, I made them worse. I made things worse when I tried to pretend I was okay. So, I hid myself in the bonus room or out at a nature preserve near our house. It gets awkward when you start to appear so physically ill. Sometimes healthy people don't know how to act. Sometimes they feel uncomfortable because there is nothing they can do.

SURELY, I WOULD GET in touch with my doctor tomorrow, and everything would be straightened out. Surely, my mom was already getting in touch with the authorities and ready to get me out. Maybe she would finally understand just how twisted traditional medicine was and how burnt I had been. Maybe we would make a breakthrough from this.

After our 8:30 p.m. snack, we took our bedtime medications, acid reflux pills, and stool softeners (lots of those were had).

Our nurse hung around to get the last vitals for the night, and to monitor us while we brushed our teeth and washed our faces. All the doors were to be kept open. Nurses would roam the halls all night to make sure that no one was out of bed.

My roommate, Katie, knew the drill. She waited until the coast was clear and power-walked the short length of our room, back and forth, as she shared more about herself. I excitedly joined her. I love walking, movement, stretching. There was an eerie familiarity about her. As uncomfortable as I was being here, I felt comfortable with her. She had nothing to hide and at least we could relate in a few ways—mostly being that we both had a record of being hard on ourselves. It felt good to connect with someone without being "the victim" or the one who was entirely falling apart. We were both falling apart and in that moment, it was OK.

This was one of many treatments for Katie. She had been all around the country in over twenty different treatment centers, and apparently, this was one of the better ones.

Katie turned our thermostat down to what I called the "Antarctica" setting right before we went to bed. She got really hot at night, especially on days she increased calories. Eventually, the nurses got an inflatable warming blanket to lay on top of me. It looked like the Michelin Man and was powered by an extremely loud motor. I was still freezing until the last week of my stay.

I barely fell asleep before the nurse was in again to take our vitals before the sun came up. My blood sugar was in the sixties, and I had to drink some apple juice ASAP.

Katie knew every single nurse on a personal level. She knew the drill so well that she could do everything without being asked. Katie was a nurse herself, so she understood everything they were doing. I watched in amazement as she went through all the motions while still remaining half asleep. She was clearly not a morning person. I ventured to try to learn from her before the day really began. She wasn't afraid to tell me I was making her anxious by asking questions about the meals. I respected her for speaking her mind and setting boundaries.

We took turns brushing teeth and bathing before breakfast.

There was a chair in the shower. I didn't understand why until I realized there were others in our group that were wheelchair-bound. Was I so weak to be held here, at this level? How could I have let it get so far without realizing?

Maybe my blood sugar *was* lower than it really needed to be, or than what was really optimal. Maybe my internal organs were shutting down, and I *did* need this help.

---

1. Hypoglycemia: https://www.mayoclinic.org/diseases-conditions/hypoglycemia/symptoms-causes/syc-20373685
2. Insulin Resistance: https://my.clevelandclinic.org/health/diseases/22206-insulin-resistance

3

The Start of Change

We made our way out to the common room. A couple of kids were getting their blood drawn. A preppy-looking girl was blow drying her hair (*for who?* I wondered). Another was working on what looked like her twentieth hemp bracelet (literally).

There was one male. His name was Zach. He was a gentleman, holding doors and looking out for others. He was quiet and seemed to enjoy reading quite a bit—not just because he was stuck in the hospital.

I looked around for a girl with blue hair whom I had noticed on my second day in the EDU. She was nowhere in sight. *Had she escaped? Did her family get her out?* I later connected the dots: she was getting intermittent shock therapy treatments.

Katie readily perched herself on what was clearly her designated spot. She was on the couch right in front of the wall of windows that peered out to a world from which we were prohibited and completely shut off—we were invisible to it. She had a pillow arranged for her comfort, particularly for her long legs. Her pant legs were always rolled up. She wiggled herself into a contorted but comfortable and seemingly well-known position. She fell asleep for short naps in between our meals, snacks, vitals, crafts, and therapies. She was also in charge of movies. She had a giant collection of DVDs, and she was pretty great at looking out for the group.

I made a beeline to the phone and immediately called my doctor, even before my mom. No answer. No answer from my parents either. How could this be? What was everyone doing? Have I mentioned I felt invisible? This differed from feeling forgotten. I felt *erased*. Like I must have been too great of a burden, or too painful of a thought for my doctor or family to deal with.

"Rebekah Farmer?"

That's me.

"We need to take some labs. Which arm do you prefer?"

I sat down from my halfway perched position on the chair and promptly held out my right arm.

Ever since I started getting really sick, it seemed nearly impossible to draw blood. I had already had countless emergency room visits to stabilize electrolytes in which I was stabbed, pricked, and prodded over twenty consecutive times, and still stumped even the best lab technicians. My veins rolled, and they were all so tiny. I had very poor circulation. They would bring hot packs, warm blankets, more water in case I was dehydrated... I hadn't had a successful blood draw in over two years by this time.

These guys were different. They drew blood on the first attempt. Though it took longer and started to slow quickly, they always got what they needed.

I was relieved. The last thing I needed was to make another scene. It was nice to know how to be handled. It was nice to not be a surprise. They were familiar with the state I was in.

I was tiny, and I was constantly cold. Though at the time I was, for the most part, oblivious to these facts. I was so used to pain that it almost helped me to get by each passing day. It numbed me in so many ways. Dull pain and coldness were distractions from the sharp inflictions of fear, shame, and emotional detachment.

I used to sleep on ice packs and do extreme yoga poses because it required all of my energy and focus. I felt more resilient afterwards. "Eustress", aka *good stress*, was my number one coping method. To some degree, it was beneficial. But I took it too far, much as I had done with many other things in my life.

> ***eustress***
> ***[yo͞o'stres]***
> ***NOUN***
> ***moderate or normal psychological stress interpreted as being beneficial for the experiencer; a positive form of stress having a beneficial effect on health, motivation, performance, and emotional well-being*** [1]

After my labs were drawn, the nurses gave me a couple of vitamins. They said that I would not be getting any of my supplements back.

"May I have another glass of water?" I asked after I swallowed my chalky, horse-pill-sized multivitamin.

"You may, but you need to add it to your water log for the day."

"May I have the computer login?"

"You've not earned that privilege yet."

20 minutes later, I was called into the small room to meet with the resident doctor. She was everything I would imagine someone in charge of a place like this to be. She seemed like someone who would be very lonely out in the real world, beyond this building. She was seemingly uncompassionate, unforgiving, and barely gave me a chance to talk. That is, until I wanted to talk about medications. When she asked how I slept, I was transparent in admitting my great struggle with insomnia. She asked if I would like to try any sleep medications. Any other complaints I had about pain, digestive issues, and blood sugar issues were all met with an option to discuss medications.

What about the chiropractic adjustments that I needed? My rib slipped out of place every day. What about the trigger point massage and Gua Sha therapy? Those seemed to be the only things that could release the knots and trigger points in my back, which were as tough and tight as a chain wire fence.

"We don't have any chiropractors or massage here. You will not be able to leave the premises to get these treatments. We can't say when you will be out of here, but it is not looking any sooner than two months."

"Or what?" I asked. "You can't hold me here against my will. I'm not supposed to be here! Have you even spoken with my doctor yet?"

"We've already spoken with your doctor and your parents."

I felt like I was going to vomit. Those words were the last that I wanted to hear. I wished I had imagined them. I wished they hadn't been reached by anyone yet. I felt a sense of doom and despair creep into my spirit.

I WAS RELEASED, SPEECHLESS, and halfway in tears. I felt very warm for the first time in a long time. I could practically feel my blood boiling beneath my skin.

I did nothing but sit until breakfast was announced. I felt like Katie was keeping an eye on me, but she said nothing. She made friendly conversation with the rest of the kids. We already had a vibe and unspoken understanding. I was grateful for that.

My first breakfast was a smaller version of the same breakfast I would have every day for the following month. Scrambled eggs with cheese and a side of salsa. Two pieces of wheat toast, one butter packet. Today was real butter. I wish I had known to really cherish it, because the rest of my stay was filled with margarine.

There was no way to make it out of here without eating 75% carbohydrates minimum per day. I did my absolute best at making my first meal of the day as protein rich and fat heavy as possible, in order to stabilize blood sugars throughout the day. My two "optional condiments" of choice were two packs of butter, until they finally declared that butter was to be counted towards macros for the day... My body was screaming for fat. I was thirsty not just for more water, but for more fat! They removed peanut butter from the free condiments as well. I was the only one trying to eat as much fat as possible, and my approach wasn't subtle.

The other breakfast options had me shaking my head. They were entertaining to me because they didn't seem like something that would hold anyone over. It was sugar on sugar. Pancakes, yogurt with granola and fruit... They didn't have to count jelly towards any macronutrient. It seems like sugar was a total freebie here. You'd *think* they would be more diligent about tracking it, considering the fact that they tested our blood sugar eight times per day. You'd *think* the standard diabetic diet (which is what they served at the EDU) would make an effort to reduce the foods that had the greatest glycemic index.

ONE OF THE NURSES greatly empathized with me and my situation. She approached me as I sat alone and apart from the others, who were working on more hemp bracelets and puzzles.

All she had to do was walk up to me and give me one look that implied "I'm listening" and possibly also "I know this sucks"; the floodgates opened wide.

"I don't have an eating disorder. All of this food makes me sick. I can feel all of my autoimmune symptoms flaring up already..."

"This is the standard diabetic diet," she explained. "This has always been the protocol here in the eating disorder unit. I know it's not what you are used to and it may *not* be the best, but we really are doing our best to take care of you."

She let me use the telephone even though nobody was supposed to be using it. Cognitive Behavioral Therapy (CBT) was about to begin in a couple of minutes.

I made another round of my phone calls with no response. I was officially feeling angry, abandoned, and hurt.

"I know you aren't planning on being here for long, but I think you should join the classes with everyone else while you are here."

I snuck in a little late and took a seat with my giant untouched binder. I was given a handout, and I followed along, filling in the blanks.

We were asked to describe the different ways we felt when in larger groups of people who didn't have the same struggles that we did. Almost everyone had something to contribute that I could also relate to, though I didn't want to admit it. Perhaps this wasn't a total waste of time. It was nice to be understood. A small part of me wanted to speak up, and to contribute as well. But I was still too shaken up. Truth be told, I needed to be broken down, and I was on the brink of it.

The very next topic was about tension within close relationships in our families, and how easy it was to have misunderstandings. In a moment, all of my emotional boundaries, walls, and guards were dismantled. I had long awaited a safe space to explain how deeply misunderstood I felt, and how much it interfered with every aspect of my life—including relationships with others, with myself, and with God.

I spoke out about how misunderstood I felt, even in that moment as I bore my wounded spirit to these total strangers. I openly admitted that I couldn't believe it had gotten this bad. Autoimmune disease is invisible, and that makes it so much harder to bear or talk about. It's awkward. It feels like a burden to share. But it's such a burden to carry alone.

It felt good to express myself to people that didn't have any control over me. I had to be selective and careful with my doctors, family, and friends. Here, it didn't matter. Things couldn't get much worse. While this was a somewhat uncomposed and sloppy emotional release, it was still a step forward. It was an action of healing. It was the opposite of isolation.

Invisible disease is lonely and scary. It makes you question how much is real and how much is in your head, or manifested from your thoughts versus rooted elsewhere. Regardless of where it starts, it infects the spirit. It's not fair to receive less compassion than someone with a visible disease, but that's usually the case. Lyme disease, Crohn's disease, ADHD, many autoimmune diseases, and mood disorders are invisible, yet life-threatening and most certainly life-altering.

I felt embarrassed to talk about a burden that someone couldn't see. I could sense that it made others uncomfortable. What people *could* see was that I was severely underweight. So that's what they ran with.

> ***Invisible disabilities, also known as Hidden Disabilities or Non-visible Disabilities, are disabilities that are not immediately apparent, are typically chronic illnesses and conditions that significantly impair normal activities of daily living.***[2]

Another snack time already—my third apple of the day. This was already more fruit than I had consumed the entire previous year. The other younger kids were in their school session, and Katie and I had an early start to OCT (Occupational Therapy) after our pre-lunch snacks.

I opted to pair my apple with plain yogurt and peanut butter. I felt it a wise plan, made from the day before. I would have asked for an apple cutter much sooner if I had known this was the second of at least a hundred apples to be had in the next thirty days. I won't say I got tired of those apples. They were mostly good, and I enjoy eating. But after a while, my jaw was tired of chewing fiber and mush.

Occupational therapy was fun. Both therapists were laid back, fun-loving, and understanding. They both also had British accents. The male approached me in multiple instances to inquire about more personal details. What was going on with me? What would I do once I figured out all the autoimmune issues? He inquired as if there were no doubt that I would make it through. I actually never communicated to him what I had tried to communicate to all the other staff—that I wasn't really supposed to be here. He must have read up on me or spoken to another nurse. Once again, I felt heard and known, and that was *really* cool.

SOON ENOUGH, IT WAS lunch. After lunch, we travelled to another room outside the unit to play a board game and do a craft. I could get down with this type of therapy.

We were asked to create a visual representation of something that felt safe, something that brought back a good memory.

The first thing that came to mind is what I painted with watercolors on a thick piece of white construction paper:

A sunrise, over a steep grassy hill, with a large blue fleece blanket obstructing part of the view. It was a dewy, carefree morning.

The photo I painted the picture from

We had both met at our first job at Chick-fil-A. Both of us were night owls. Both of us had teenage angst. Blah blah blah.

We used to meet up at a reservoir in our town late at night. Though we were of the opposite sex and mutually attracted to one another, we didn't hang out to play mind games or send mixed signals. We hung out to enjoy the company of one another. We didn't have to talk much. We walked. We lay down. We sometimes fell asleep. No expectations, pressure, or judgement. We didn't hang out to flirt. We enjoyed being known and just being.

That's why it came to mind. I hadn't felt *known* or truly accepted since those times.

I STOPPED CALLING MY doctors and Mom.

I started to go numb and break down all at the same time. That night I really understood that there truly is nothing and no one on this planet that won't let me down, except for God. I started writing in a devotional journal my mom had got me. I jotted down many heart-cries on those pages.

I shifted my internal perspective, trying to dig deep and make sure I repented of every single thing I had been holding back. I asked God to break me down and give me the strength to fall on my knees at His throne of Grace. I didn't even know who God was, but I was asking for Him to show me. I needed Him to show me, because I was *tired of fighting.*

1. Merriam-Webster:
   https://www.merriam-webster.com/dictionary/eustress
2. Invisible Disability:
   https://www.disabled-world.com/disability/types/invisible/

4

Different Disorders, Similar Souls

One evening while walking to the meal room for dinner, I noticed the door to the next unit was open. They had at least twice, if not three times, as many kids over there. "That's for people with binge eating disorders," Katie shared.

The more time I spent observing and listening to the people who were patients in this ward, the more I realized we were all worlds apart but still had so much in common. The concept of an eating disorder shifted for me. I never set out to get thin or starve myself—but through a lot of wonky, disturbing, unpredictable circumstances, my relationship with food had absolutely become unhealthy. I *did* have a concern for the types and quality of food that I was eating. Was it unnecessary or unimportant? No, and in fact, it *is* very important. But the fact remains that my relationship with food had become tense. I did not feel I could eat intuitively or trust the cravings or signals my body would send me. Those were all chaotic.

Do I have an eating disorder? Maybe this is where I need to be. I searched my heart of hearts on this matter—not just during this time in the eating disorder unit, but for years after the fact, and even now as I share my testimony.

Once, in 7th grade, I tried to make myself throw up. My sister heard me in the shower and told my parents. Good thing too, because they confirmed my quick realization that this was not a solution to lose the uncomfortable pubescent weight I was failing to adjust to. I knew it was something that would destroy my body and would not be sustainable. I continued to struggle as most do during puberty. I received unwanted attention from older guys, and I wanted to hide. It was then, in the 7th grade, when I had felt the most insecure, and mood disorders started to take over. I was diagnosed with ADHD, anxiety, insomnia, depression, OCD, and narcolepsy.

I was then prescribed Adderall, Clonazepam, and Ambien. Before filling these prescriptions, I asked if it would be difficult to get off of them when I decided to. "They're not addictive, and you can safely take them long term." I was told.

Benzopadines should not be taken for more than 30 days. I took all three at increasing dosages for a little over 13 years.

They helped me to function, somewhat, in the beginning. But they stole so much of my personality. In the end, they played a large role in damaging my gut, neurotransmitters, adrenals, hormones, and more. I was addicted. I was dependent. I was under the impression that I had no other options.

Though I did not attempt to starve myself or purge after that first incident, I didn't love the body that I had. I struggled with digestive issues and gathered it was normal enough to be in pain after eating. My relationship with food wasn't bad, but also wasn't great. I couldn't help but take note of the increasing sensitivities I was developing. I naturally progressed towards Keto, while never eating anything like a Standard American Diet. I am so grateful that my mom never kept much sugar in the house.

I had pop and fruit roll-ups at my friends' houses, but never at home or from my own packed lunch box. Occasionally, my mom would let my sister and I choose toaster strudels from the grocery store. I could never eat just two… I always made a second batch. Though I enjoyed the sugar, I never craved it like I did salty, buttery foods. Now I understand my adrenals were shot. I needed salt, and a consistent and reliable source of fuel for energy, for my starving body and brain.

Many of my issues (digestive, mood, and pain) seemed to start right after my family moved, when I was starting 6th grade. I started my period the day we drove a moving truck from Michigan to North Carolina. It was an emotionally heavy day. My father, sister, and I lived in a hotel for a short time, trying out new schools and finding a house. We moved twice in the same state within the same year, and I felt no desire to put down new roots. I had an incredible childhood in Michigan and I didn't want to move on.

Sure enough, I developed some strong friendships in North Carolina. My parents pulled me out of private school after a particularly hard year of peer pressure. At one point, I was taping down my breasts to avoid unwanted attention from older guys. I started homeschooling again, but at a bookstore with other students to attend smaller-sized classes with. My childhood best friend and I wrote letters, and continued to visit each Spring until graduation. With time, we grew apart. It was hard.

I was with my high school sweetheart for three years before a very painful breakup. This was my first long-term relationship. Sure, we were young, but love is love.

At the brink of the breakup, he spread rumors about me to all of our shared friends. I got anonymous messages online on a regular basis like "Go kill yourself", "Holocaust whore", and other cruel things that really brought me down.

I had already lost weight due to taking Adderall, but this heartbreak triggered something inside of me even more intense than the chronic C. Difficile infection that I more often talk about.

I was numb, and I was totally wired. I stayed up for five days at a time on a regular basis and still wouldn't feel any need to go to sleep.

I would go explore abandoned warehouses, get lost in the woods, watch the sunrise at the reservoir, and do other things that were pleasant distractions from reality. I never weighed myself or even gave a second thought to the fact that I was losing rapid amounts of weight until my family brought it up. Before I knew it, I was at Goodwill in the children's section trying to find jeans that didn't fall off of me.

Five years later, he apologized to me for everything. He is married now, and I am happy for him. I am grateful to have concluded in peace.

I didn't have an eating disorder. I had mood disorders, and I was traumatized. I was being bullied. I was grieving. I had a grudge against my parents for pulling me away from everything I knew to be home.

It made me angry that my family tried confronting me about an eating disorder, only because I was upset that they didn't realize there was so much more to it. I needed someone to talk to and help me—not with eating, but about trauma and rumors and heartbreak and peer pressure. I was overwhelmed.

WITH TIME COMES HEALING and I put on some healthy weight again. But I was not healthy. My health continued to decline while I worked at Whole Foods and lived off of Skinny Pop, Arctic Zero, and star-shaped grain-free sweet potato cookies with chocolate chips. I would occasionally treat myself to cinnamon raisin Ezekiel bread to slather with Kerrygold butter. I am horrified when I think about how little protein I ate during this time. Eating two eggs for breakfast on a weekend was considered more than enough. I didn't understand the importance of protein. I only understood that sugar and certain seed oils were no good. I loved and ate plenty of healthy fat. I had no concept or understanding of antinutrients.

I was living aimlessly. I was extremely dependent on Adderall, clonazepam, and Ambien.

I was a different person, unsure who I was or what I was created for.

5

Clinic Exit Strategy

Chronic Lyme Disease

I WASN'T VERY SURPRISED when I was diagnosed with it. I was dealing with suffocation attacks and chronic fatigue. My brain felt like a steamed vegetable 24/7. I had heard of Lyme disease, but never imagined I'd have to face it. I also never imagined I'd be dealing with the more serious symptoms. If I'm being honest, I was always on the fence about whether I believed it was as bad as I had heard.

All the Lyme literate doctors said that I needed their treatments indefinitely. IVs, ozone therapy, expensive supplements, hyperbaric chamber sessions. I didn't stay for long though, because I had a strong conviction to walk away. I noticed that all the other patients had already accepted defeat. They were ready and committed to a life of IV treatments and identifying with a disease. I think these treatment centers and Lyme literate doctors have a lot to offer, I truly do. *But nothing can heal someone from a disease that they've already succumbed to in their hearts or minds.*

Even though I was dealing with non-epileptic seizures and was completely beside myself, I felt peace about walking away from those clinics. It wasn't sustainable in the least. I would rather listen to my heart and walk away than spend money I didn't have on treatments that didn't guarantee success. It looked more like a life sentence, or a matrimony to a clinic and disease, than true healing or freedom.

My mom once told me, "If it doesn't give you peace, it's not from God." I finally knew what she meant. I had no peace about this place as much as I *wanted* to find a solution or even a plan.

I continued to brainstorm and troubleshoot with Functional Medicine Doctors, Chiropractors, and neurologists. After so long, this mostly was just running in circles. Eventually, I ended up at UNC, by accident (or by God's grand design).

Snacks blurred into meals. Days blurred into weeks. I learned how to somewhat enjoy my time in this weird place. I could definitely appreciate living in baggy sweatshirts and stretchy pants, not seeing my reflection in the mirror, and having an excuse to read and journal a lot more. Every time I thought about going back home, I became very anxious. I had let go of something that I didn't want to have to carry again. I couldn't put a name to it, but my breathing was easier. Sure, I was in pain. I was in *a lot* of pain. But somewhere in my soul, I was resting where I had long been restless. It felt so good to be powerless—to not be micromanaging every moment of every day (though I tried to).

Every day became more about surrender and addressing my heart posture. My attitude determined the outcome of the entire day. Was I going to walk in bitterness and fear, or trust and hope?

My roommate managed to gain 15 lbs and was discharged. The others had multiple visitors for lunch and dinner, who even stayed after to play games. I felt really left out and insecure, seeing all these supportive families and not even talking to my own. I was so happy for Katie. It was hard to see her go. She had a boyfriend she had spoken of who showed up that day. He picked her up in the air and swung her around with a fairy tale movie-type of hug. My heart wrenched inside of me as I thought of all the relationships that had fallen to pieces around me over the past few years. It was not all my fault. People change.

But it was largely my fault, for I had changed. I was grieving the life and experiences I had lost to disease. I was angry and felt wounded. But this past month, I had a chance to process. I was turning over a new page in a new chapter of life. I was ready to wash out the bitter taste leftover from regret.

Though I had spent the last month consuming copious sugar, carbs, antinutrients, and seed oils, in some ways, I was undeniably starting to feel much more stable. My blood sugars and electrolytes were more stable than they were when I was admitted and I wasn't in *constant* fight-or-flight mode. I was sleeping four hours some nights, which was an improvement. I was no longer needing to be treated at *emergency room* level. I was ready to get out of there, especially with my roommate moving on.

I confronted the doctor, who finally admitted that I had "*exhibited 0 signs of an eating disorder*". These words came out of her own mouth, but she was unwilling to repeat them later on in the presence of my parents.

I checked myself out AMA (Against Medical Advice), deviating the standard requirement of months of step-down treatments, first in residential and then outpatient centers. This wasn't easy to work out. In fact, I had spent most of my earned computer privileges looking into residential options covered by insurance. My options were slim, and I needed to get back to my FMD and chiropractor. I just wanted to do what was right. I wanted to move forward, not backward. I had so many opinions to consider about what was really best for me.

I was to go home and continue with eating disorder certified nutritionists and therapists.

6

Back to Before

I DIDN'T EXPECT THE emotions that surfaced as soon as I stepped into the car with my mom the day I left.

Up in the unit, I was anxious about getting out. My mom was gentle, patient, and kind. But I knew she was also still blinded and brainwashed by the lies they had fed her for the intense month prior. I knew that what she envisioned the future to be was not what I needed, and that it was going to cause issues. I knew that there was so much misunderstanding that had to surface.

I was bottling up all of this trauma and legitimate pain. It was nice that I didn't have to deal with it during my time at the unit, but I wanted it to be acknowledged at home, too. I wanted the same encouragement and support the others had received from their families, and I wanted it badly. I felt very bitter and angry that I didn't have it. I felt abandoned. I had watched as the weeks passed, with full crowds on visitor evenings. My heart had sunk inside of me. My stomach would tighten up and feel sour.

Nothing compares to the hurt felt when you know that you've become a great burden and disappointment to those who you want to make the proudest. I wanted my family to understand that battle I had been fighting. It wasn't easy! *And the truth is they may never fully understand, as I will also never understand what* they *went through.*

Disease and chronic illness may sometimes be "invisible", but it doesn't go unnoticed. It affects everyone around you. It's awkward to bear. Should I expose it or protect the ones I love from heartache? They don't have manuals written for these things that are sometimes even romanticized on social media—as if it were something to place on a pedestal. Let's get real. Chronic illness is ugly. It tears apart relationships and tears down dreams. It strips so many of joy and irreplaceable, invaluable life experiences. But praise God, He delivers and redeems. God carries us through all that is lost and cannot be recovered, and lifts us up by His Grace into a Love and a life that we couldn't have even imagined. That's what He does. It's in His nature. It's through this process that I came to know this to be true in my heart of hearts.

> "*'For I will restore health to you, and your wounds I will heal,' declares the Lord, 'because they have called you an outcast: 'It is Zion, for whom no one cares!'*"
>
> —Jeremiah 30:17

> "*Instead of your shame, there shall be a double portion; instead of dishonor, they shall rejoice in their lot; therefore, in their land*

they shall possess a double portion; they shall have everlasting joy."

—Isaiah 61:7

"*And the Lord restored the fortunes of Job, when he had prayed for his friends. And the Lord gave Job twice as much as he had before.*"

—Job 42:10

"*And after you have suffered a little while, the God of all grace, who has called you to his eternal glory in Christ, will himself restore, confirm, strengthen, and establish you.*"

—Peter 5:10

"*Come, let us return to the Lord; for he has torn us, that he may heal us; he has struck us down, and he will bind us up.*"

—Hosea 6:1

I WAS ANGRY THAT I was still being required to work with eating disorder specialists. I was angry that my family thought I'd somehow be on board with all of this now and that my issues would dissolve into thin air now that I had gained weight. I was angry that nobody recognized the trauma of being held against my own will in an eating disorder unit. My ego was angry. I had a true issue and fear of being misunderstood. My rights had been trampled once again. The more I focused on what was "fair" or what "should have been", the angrier I felt.

From my parents' perspective, their second daughter had escaped the grips of death and seemed to be much more physically stable. And that is the truth. I wish I had spent more time thanking the Lord for protecting me, carrying me, and always providing.

They didn't seem interested in the details of autoimmune issues—the invisible things.

As soon as I got home, I felt as if nothing had changed. There was the same toxic dynamic, frustration, and anxiety about what was really at the root of my problems and what it would take to navigate and find healing.

My bedroom had been ransacked. All my supplements (thousands of dollars' worth) had been taken.

I made an appointment with my chiropractor and functional medicine doctor ASAP.

I couldn't wait to talk with someone about boundaries—or the lack thereof. I was triggered, traumatized, and exhausted.

I WAS HALF EXPECTING my phone to be full of missed calls and text messages. I had under ten of both combined. I felt lonelier and more misunderstood than I did going into the place. I felt like everyone's true colors were showing. It was dreadful.I didn't know what I was looking forward to anymore... I lost sight of goals and dreams because they didn't seem realistic to have. But I looked forward to every new morning. Because the morning is full of new mercies and fresh starts.

> "*The steadfast love of the Lord never ceases; his mercies never come to an end; they are new every morning; great is your faithfulness.*"
>
> —Lamentations 3:22-23

I looked forward to bedtime, because even though I didn't sleep much, it was an escape. I was guaranteed privacy, silence, and essential oils diffused next to my face for hours.

My life had become very small, and life itself seemed to have escaped me entirely. The world wasn't slowing down, and everything and everyone I loved was out there in it. I needed to shift my perspective. I needed hope.

I needed Jesus.

7

It's the Inside That Counts

Fall, 2017

"You look so much better!" Everyone at my chiropractor and doctors' offices raved. It took me right back to the family trip to Michigan, when it seemed like the only things anyone could ever care about were outward appearances. As long as my appearance made *them* feel comfortable, all was well enough.

Truthfully, I felt even worse. A couple of weeks after I was home from the hospital, I broke out in the worst rash I've ever had in my entire life. It started on my face, then I noticed it took over my entire back. I was horrified! The traditional medicine doctor prescribed me some ointment, which did nothing.

This was what many refer to as the "Keto rash", which also has a lot to do with oxalate dumping. I had never experienced this before, even with years of being on a ketogenic diet, because I had never loaded up on so much sugar and anti-nutrients in such a short timeframe as I did in the hospital.

It was a loaded, unprepared, and uncomfortable purge. It lasted for about three months.

> ***oxalate***
> ***['äksəˌlāt]***
> ***NOUN***
> ***chemistry***
> ***a salt or ester of oxalic acid.***
> ***any salt or ester of oxalic acid, occurring in plants, especially spinach, rhubarb, and certain other vegetables and nuts, and capable of forming an insoluble salt with calcium and interfering with its absorption by the body.***[1]

No dietitian, therapist, functional medicine doctor, or even open threats about eating disorder treatments could convince me to voluntarily eat sugar every day.

It was as simple as choosing between heart palpitations, brain fog, severe fatigue, nausea, anxiety, temperature fluctuation, more inflammation, and bad skin OR enough energy to get out of bed, go for walks outside, more tolerable digestive issues, and better skin...

Even if none of those things were optimal either way, the starkest difference was in my mood. Our brain and body, when running primarily on glucose, in itself creates oxidative stress—which often gives way to inflammation. In my circumstances, it gave way to apathy, depression, fear, doubt, systemic inflammation (joints, mood, skin, gut, energy), and feeling generally overwhelmed. Becoming fat adapted and shifting to using fat as a primary fuel source is like removing a heavy weight, along with providing anti-inflammatory benefits. Fat adaption is *un*inflammatory.

Me with the weight I had gained from the EDU

Even still being under 100 lbs, I had good strength. There were times I felt like a noodle, and there were times I could feel my small muscles supporting me. The more I ate fat and meat, the stronger I felt. I could feel the switch between catabolism & fight/flight to rest & digest (parasympathetic), and recovery moving from sugar-burning to fat burning.

catabolism
[kəˈtabəˌlizəm]
NOUN
biology
the breakdown of complex molecules in living organisms to form simpler ones, together with the release of energy; destructive metabolism.[2]

Fight or Flight (Fight-or-Flight) is the combination of physical responses to fear that prepare you to react to a dangerous situation in one of two ways—to fight (fight) or to flee (flight). Your body has specific responses, such as increased heart rate, increased blood pressure, increased adrenaline flow, etc.

The difference between the sympathetic and parasympathetic nervous system is that the sympathetic nervous system functions to mobilize the body's fight-or-flight response, while the parasympathetic nervous system functions to control the homeostasis of the body.[3]

I kept pads of butter on my bedside table to nibble on right before bedtime, in the middle of the night when I woke due to cortisol, and first thing in the morning. This helped keep my central nervous system in a supported place. Being at such a low body fat percentage meant I needed to keep the dietary fat coming in consistently. My body had to stay out of starvation mode. So, sending that signal was of the utmost importance to keep cortisol down. I quickly realized that it was more about the signal than any specific amount of fat. If I could just reassure my body, my central nervous system, and my brain, I could mitigate so much stress and start to get deeper sleep—which has its own cascade of benefits and improvements.

I LOST ALMOST ALL the weight I had gained within a couple of weeks. I knew I was pretty good at Keto without counting macros, but this was too much.

I was constantly anxious as I felt my mom watch me cook or eat in the kitchen. I ate the same thing every day for at least four months after the hospital. It was what I told my dietician I was eating, and I didn't have the desire nor mental capacity to even try to change anything up for variety. I was exhausted, and I was still getting nowhere with my functional medicine doctor.

For breakfast, I ate ground beef or ground pork with an egg cracked in the middle of it, served on top of baby spinach and a fourth of an avocado.

I usually followed up breakfast with *too many* coconut manna fat bombs. Coconut manna eventually became a stumbling block—something I would binge on in my walk-in closet. I was ashamed of eating it by the spoonful in front of anyone. So, I hid. And in my hiding, my relationship with another food became estranged and unhealthy. I shouldn't have been ashamed to enjoy food like I was. The eating disorder treatment left me feeling more uneasy around food and in my thoughts about eating than ever before.

For lunch, I had a spinach salad with a poached egg, sardines, and another fourth of an avocado.

For dinner, I had meat. I always looked forward to dinner, as it was my largest portion of protein. I ate a lot of raw meat during this time, and I would isolate myself to the formal dining room to avoid concern from my family. If I'm being completely honest, I was a little concerned about myself. Why was I craving this raw meat so much every day? I would sometimes pair it with mustard and a duck egg. It was *so* refreshing. I can't quite describe how satisfying it was, but it was quenching a deep thirst that my body had for those nutrients.

THE DYNAMIC AT HOME had become very toxic. My mom would sometimes confine herself to her bedroom all day, and I spent way too much time in the kitchen. If I wasn't in the kitchen, I was in bed or outside at a nature park trying to escape the chaos of reality.

I think back to the state I was in and ask myself if I should have pushed myself the way that I did. At many times, I shouldn't have been driving. I was not medically stable, but I was also losing my mind and hope. I was greatly distressed and discouraged. There were few things that brought me solace, and being out in the middle of a large, lush forest was one of them—as it always had been.

I would return to the nature park that I was planning to have my wedding at just a little while ago.

The lush forest trails I used to roam back in NC

Back then, I was engaged and working full time in real estate. I was essentially planning my own wedding when the suffocation attacks started. That's when I decided to get off my medications and get to the root of the problem, even if it killed me. The medications weren't helping anymore. I pushed him away deep down, hoping he would fight for me because I was terrified he would leave me for my medical issues. I was afraid, and I so wanted to know that I was not alone. But he left when I pushed him away, and I moved back in with my parents.

In hindsight, I'm grateful for how everything went down because we were not ready to be married and it was not God's will.

I walked the same trails that I used to run, to cope with the stress of these things I was living with that I did not understand. I longed to go back to that time that I just did not understand. It was just a passing feeling, enough to sweep under the rug. I was far beyond that ability now.

One day, I tripped on a root and gashed my knee wide open, down to the bone. I had blood gushing down the front of my legs and walked a mile back to my car without even wincing.

I remember at that moment realizing just how numb I was. Nothing could rattle me or shake me. I was burnt out. Numbness was my default.

My weight continued to drop at rapid rates. I was wearing fleece leggings underneath my size 00 pants again to look somewhat normal. I was worried.

I started to spend three times as much time in the kitchen, cooking up every single keto recipe I'd ever dreamt of making. At one point, I was eating 6000 calories per day and still losing weight. This is when I created my first dairy-free ice cream recipe, because ice cream was the easiest thing to eat in large amounts.

My eating habits and relationship with food started to become a little hectic. Breakfast occasionally turned into a full-on buffet until it was lunchtime. I could tell my blood sugars started to become less and less stable as I ate around the clock. I was having more cravings, but they did not seem false. I felt my body literally starving. *Was this all emotional hunger? How could my gut be so compromised? Did I need to eat carbs again?*

1. Oxalates: https://www.webmd.com/diet/foods-high-in-oxalates
2. Catabolism: https://www.britannica.com/science/catabolism
3. Stress Response (Flight or Flight): https://www.health.harvard.edu/staying-healthy/understanding-the-stress-response

8

Gut Pains

Early Spring, 2018

Fall came and went. The Holidays were a blur. I was detached and dissociated.

One steamy and sultry spring morning, I finished up my second breakfast (this was normal these days, as I was still trying to keep the weight on) with Nori sheets baked with nutritional yeast. Just another "Keto" snack, while being low carb—it also didn't provide the nutrients my body was starved for. I hadn't yet adopted the concept of "nutrient density" within my way of eating. I only concerned myself with *staying away from too much of the bad stuff, so long as I was still comfortable.*

I almost always followed meals with walking, because I saw a strong correlation in stabilized blood sugars with it. Even if it was just ten minutes of walking, I had found it made a positive impact on digestion as well.

So, I went out for a walk, when exactly halfway around the block I had to make a quick dash into the woods (thank goodness North Carolina has a ton of trees everywhere). I felt like my guts were spilling out of me. I "air dried" as best I could (too much poison ivy and risk of choosing the wrong leaf) and casually popped back out of the woods and onto the road. Not a whole minute later, I was literally sitting on the ground using all my might to not crap myself in front of all of my neighbors. I started to cry. A 26-year-old baby, with poopy pants and all.

I called my mom and asked her to pick me up, and to please bring a towel. By the time she arrived, I had made a mess—literally.

She didn't even ask what happened. I didn't know what was happening. This was not MCT oil "diarrhea pants". This was some next-level crap! She was clearly fed up and exasperated.

These occurrences progressed over the next couple of months. I spent a lot of time either walking in nature preserves, or at doctors' offices. I started carrying baby wipes with me. My weight started to drop more rapidly than ever before. My clothes were falling off of me again, and I was still eating more and more. The burden of trying to keep up physically, emotionally, and mentally was too much. It was too much for me, my family, and my close friends. I was fighting in my own strength again, which I had set out to not do upon leaving the EDU, but it just seemed to fall right into place—almost as if there were no other options.

Every previous relationship was either non-existent or now had a whole new set of boundaries. I didn't know what I was hoping for anymore. All I wanted was one day without pain, chaos, and sorrow.

The weight loss put extra strain on the family dynamics. Everyone thought it was my own doing, and entirely intentional. I didn't have time to worry about the constant diarrhea. I can't put into words the depth or degree of trauma I was constantly dealing with. There were only brief glimpses of hope and peace—usually when out in nature, away from others. Occasionally, the Lord would speak through a stranger at the gym or a grocery store. I knew I was not alone, even though I felt it—achingly so. I attributed a lot of the weight loss to stress and being in fight/flight mode.

FINALLY, MY FMD RAN a fecal test. I was diagnosed with chronic C. Diff.

Another piece to the puzzle—a large one at that. I felt like this could be the answer. If I could get this under control, I'd be able to get back on my feet and start gaining momentum again.

I'd be able to gain weight, strength, and reduce the toxic load of malnourishment both physically and emotionally on myself *and everyone around me.*

9

Remedy Trials

Clostridium Difficile - C. Diff

I WAS RELIEVED. IT wasn't all in my head. It was something I couldn't have guessed. In fact, I had never heard of it before. A quick Google search confirmed the severity of C. Diff and its effects.

> ***Clostridium difficile (also known as: C. difficile, C. diff)***
>
> ***Infection of the large intestine (colon) caused by the bacteria Clostridium difficile. Long-term use of antibiotics reduces the normal bacterial population in the intestine and triggers the C. difficile overgrowth in the intestine.***
>
> ***Urgent medical attention is usually recommended in severe cases by healthcare providers.***

Certain types can be dangerous or life-threatening if untreated. [1]

I scrolled through pages of blogs, images, studies—most of which should have made me more uneasy, but it didn't. I felt like a burden had been lifted. It felt good to have a diagnosis, and to have a better understanding of the beast I was facing. I didn't want to take antibiotics, but these were the only option given (no surprise there). Considering the situation and urgency, I bit the bullet. I didn't have much to lose, literally.I took the prescribed antibiotics and hoped for the best. The doctor seemed to think these were going to totally inoculate it. At least I would be out of this storm soon, I thought, and then I could focus on healing from the autoimmune components, Lyme Disease, and relationships with my family and close friends. I started dreaming about a normal, productive life lived with others and not frequently visiting doctors.

I often felt like I was stuck in a deep sleep, living in a nightmare. I would have moments where I felt I was finally waking up to a brighter, lighter reality—and I was ready to shake it all off and start fresh. But I would always be sucked back into it with even more weight than before. This was a long, nightmarish reality with little known escape. Life was heavy as I literally wasted away.

Escape was just the small moments where the pain was less. Escape was numbness. It wasn't true healing or freedom—it was just chances to barely catch my breath while I was above water for a moment. More often than not, I was in a perpetual battle with disease, with my belief systems, with trying to convince those closest to me of who I was and what I was truly going through or what I truly needed. I was battling with God. I never did stop crying out to Him. That, to me, would have been giving up.

I finished the first round of antibiotics and made another appointment with my doctor to retest for Clostridium Difficile. I don't think I've disliked anything more than at-home stool kits. It has to be fresh when dropped off. Of course, the times I needed to provide a sample were the *rare* occasions that I was not having diarrhea. So it goes.

I tested positive again. Now I was just extra wiped out after taking antibiotics for two weeks.

I explained I had been through many rounds of antibiotics in my past and was probably resistant to many of them. This didn't matter to the doctor. I'm not sure if they even heard what I had explained. Onto the next round, per standard protocol.

I tried every antibiotic that had been proven effective against Clostridium Difficile, each three times (I skipped the last two rounds, and that had to be good enough). I was clearly resistant. At this point, I felt as if anything thriving in my gut had a mind and an agenda of its own with no regard to my wellbeing. It was taking over and getting stronger.

I went through thirteen rounds of antibiotics before I was finally approved for a fecal transplant.

> ***"Fecal microbiota transplant (FMT), also known as a stool transplant, is the process of transferring fecal bacteria and other microbes from a healthy individual into another individual. FMT is an***

> ***effective treatment for Clostridiums difficile infection (CDI). For recurrent CDI, FMT is more effective than vancomycin. Approximately 2000 procedures were performed in Europe in 2019."***
> 2

I had heard of fecal transplants before from one of my relatives. It sounded crazy! Absolutely wild! And yet it made so much sense.

I had my first transplant and felt notably different the next day. It was not so much just the difference in symptoms (less diarrhea), but more so in my mood. I like to describe it as if there were another colour to my personality rainbow. If each of our personalities were composed and expressed as rainbows, mine had been not only changed but also a new color added that didn't *exist* before. It's hard to explain, but this concept and feeling would probably make a really great Netflix series.

Within another few days, something felt off again. I asked to do another stool test, halfway feeling like a bother or a hypochondriac. I tested positive. I was starting to get anxious. Weren't these supposed to be super effective? Was this punishment? What was God trying to teach me with this? I often had to remind myself that sickness does not come from God. He allows us to live in this fallen world and also provides wisdom and strength to do *all things*. But we will face trials and tribulation. I know this is what He says, but I couldn't help but feel I was being condemned. My feelings and God's truth were two separate realities and perspectives to live by. I had to choose one over the other, and very often they could not co-exist.

Displacing negative thoughts with the truth and renewing the mind is still, to this day, my number one necessity for forward motion. Every morning I *must* make time to ground myself in the Truth—His Living Word. The more I saturate myself with what God says, who He is, and His love, the less I am tossed and swayed by my feelings that are ever fleeting. Praise God for his steadfast Love.

I was approved for a second fecal transplant. This time the changes stuck... Until they didn't. One month later, I recall the very moment I knew it had taken over again. I wanted to hope for the best, but also had to be realistic. I knew this feeling probably more than any other sensation my body had experienced in life thus far. Sure enough, I tested positive and was approved for yet another fecal transplant.

I went for my third, but they were unable to finish the colonoscopy procedure prior to surgery. I was sent home and instructed to reschedule "at my earliest convenience".

---

1. C. Difficile: https://www.mayoclinic.org/diseases-conditions/c-difficile/symptoms-causes/syc-20351691
2. Fecal Transplant: https://www.ncbi.nlm.nih.gov/pmc/articles/PMC4749851/

10

It Was the Best of Times, It Was the Worst of Times

Christmastime, 2018

I was able to get into my own apartment and out of the stressful environment at home. The tension had become far too much for all of us.

I walked with an older friend who spoke encouragement and love into my life every single day. It was the highlight of my every day. I was going to the functional doctor at least three times per week.

Days turned into weeks and I continued to lose weight without any strong answers.

Isolation and condemnation became the weapon of choice that the enemy used against me. I started to panic. What if I did really have an eating disorder? Maybe it really was that simple.

December 2018

I felt dizzy and sick just thinking of how warped my days had become. I was losing structure and any form of consistency. I felt that nobody was on my side, except for my older friend. She remained a trustworthy, stable, and unchanging reinforcement. She came over one evening with her knitting materials to sit with me and wind down before bed. I was traumatized, and in a crisis not only physically but also spiritually and emotionally. The burden of my reality became too much.

I set out to gain weight above anything else. I wanted to be accepted, and I wanted to prove to others that I really was trying my best. I abandoned reason yet again from a place of fear.

I methodically set up a comfortable area in my living room to eat, for hours on end, until I could not eat any longer.

I placed towels on the couch and set up napkins and multiple bottles of water at the table.

This was not impulsive binge eating. It was intentional, organized chaos.

I started to try to harness my central nervous system in a way that I could remain calm enough to mitigate any autoimmune flare-ups while still eating at a massive surplus. At this time, I was doubling down on any biohacking trick I knew of. I took cold showers, I slept on ice packs, I used sauna, did breathing exercises, used essential oils. But there is no biohack for a deep-rooted spirit of fear.

Of course, I utilized keto treats and paleo goodies as much as possible. I did not want to fill up on empty calories or junk—I was aiming for nutrient density and biohacking my way into healing and weight gain, but I also sacrificed my conscience to take it as far as I did. I purposely used addictive components against myself, for myself. I aimed for hyper palatable foods that would suppress leptin, allowing my appetite to grow.

> ***leptin***
> ***['leptin]***
> ***NOUN***
> ***biochemistry***
> ***a protein produced by fat cells that is a hormone acting mainly in the regulation of appetite and fat storage.***[1]

One night I stayed up until the morning eating burgers, bison, sweet potatoes, avocado-cacao pudding—all while watching the "Heartland" series on Netflix. I had read the books in grade school. It was a little cheesy, and very wholesome—just what I was craving. My life felt so empty.

I missed my mom a lot. I missed my friends a lot. My heart ached when I thought about the misunderstandings and tension between us. How could these relationships ever be restored? There seemed to be only one way: for me to do what they felt was best—to be treated as if I had an eating disorder, and then live a full and happy life.

5AM, I knew that breakfast joints would be opening soon. At this point, my blood sugar had spiked and plummeted so many times, I didn't know what full or satiated meant anymore. I was running on so much adrenaline, complete exhaustion. I drove to Starbucks and was the first person to order.

I ordered enough gluten-filled entrees to host a small business conference. I was going to prove to myself once and for all that it was all in my head, that I just needed to break this unnecessary concern of "the quality of certain foods"—AKA "orthorexia". That's what I was told in the eating disorder unit, and that's what my parents believed.

orthorexia
[ˌôrTHəˈreksēə]
NOUN
an obsession with eating foods that one considers healthy.
a medical condition in which the sufferer systematically avoids specific foods in the belief that they are harmful.[2]

I brought the food home and made the bread extra toasty under the broiler. I slathered it with butter. Who doesn't love some toasty bread and butter? I finished a single side of an English muffin before I felt very uneasy and set aside the rest.

Within thirty minutes, I had severe stomach pains and a bad headache.

I wished it were as simple as overcoming my mindset. It wasn't. I was in bed for the next 48 hours, half conscious. I had "glutened" myself in hopes of proving that it was all in my head. But it wasn't. I knew that it wasn't. I missed the days that I could eat bread without consequences. I didn't think there was hope of that being possible again.

THIS BEHAVIOR CONTINUED FOR months. I was ashamed, embarrassed, and horrified. At one point, I did gain enough weight—probably more inflammation and stored glycogen/water weight to reach the triple digits (104 lbs), but it didn't stick around for more than seven days. I could not keep up with the C. Diff or the loss of nutrients that were being bound to antinutrients which, at the time, I was unaware of.

antinutrient
[ˌan(t)ēˈn(y)o͞otrēənt, ˌanˌtīˈn(y)o͞otrēənt]
NOUN
anti-nutrients (plural noun)
a natural or synthetic compound that interferes with the body's absorption of nutrients.[3]

Once again, I considered my circumstances and what I was longing for. I wanted to no longer be alone. I wanted to love someone. I wanted to live more of my life before I reached 30 years old (the age I was told to not expect to live past).

I MADE AN ACCOUNT on eHarmony. My profile couldn't have been more transparent about my situation. I did meet up with one person who seemed like quite the catch! He wanted to introduce me to his parents within the first week that we met. That evening, on our way to the restaurant, we stopped at a gas station. I started to feel nervous, and suddenly I was triggered. It was like something possessed me. I went inside the gas station and selfishly bought some white cheddar popcorn. It was something that I used to eat when I didn't have any known health problems and had no knowledge of the impact of some foods over others. It was a comfort food. I wanted to be normal. I didn't know how to deal with this shame I carried for all of my health issues. I was already so anxious about something that hadn't happened yet. I wanted to escape.

I asked if we could stop at another gas station, and I picked out some keto-chemical laden protein bar. It was delicious, but not something I felt comfortable eating more than two bites of. I knew what was going on. I knew I was triggered and not emotionally stable enough to be my best self for this person. But I was giving it my all, and I did my best to stop—though I was having a secret, internal semi breakdown. He had no idea. No one did. I had already had so much practice covering up panic attacks over the past couple of years.

Finally, at my request, we stopped at Chipotle *on the way to the restaurant* so we could get the keto bowls. I wasn't even hungry. I just wanted to feel normal before I had to face his parents, who I knew would immediately judge me for being severely underweight. I wanted to somehow prove to myself that I was normal enough within a span of 40 minutes. I wanted to feel worthy, stable, and secure. I was anything but. I was not happy with myself. I was not secure. I didn't know who I was in Christ. I didn't know who I was at all anymore. I was projecting my insecurities on those around me, whether they really realized it or not. It was wrong.

I was exhausted when we got back.

The next day, things were very awkward. He disappeared, then came back and made very strong physical passes at me, pushing me up against the wall. I stopped him and he said he didn't know what he was thinking. I went out for an errand and came back to a note. He was gone for good.

One week later, he married his ex (thanks for the notification, Facebook).

I MET ANOTHER ON eHarmony who claimed to be Christian and was also undertaking the ketogenic diet!

He lived up North. We exchanged messages back-and-forth for a couple of months. Easter came around and I had no one to spend the holiday with. My aunt Judy reached out and invited me to come visit... I was elated! I hadn't seen my cousins for over 10 years. I didn't care what they were going to think, and I wasn't really worried. We were family, after all.

That was one of the most precious trips and memories of my lifetime thus far.

My trip to Aunt Judy's; can you spot where I am in the bunch?

My aunt Judy didn't judge me. She didn't put any pressure on me to be anyone except who I was. She happily sat beside me as I ate my meals of raw meat. We took walks together, and she lovingly spoke the truth into my life. She reminded me I was not crazy for considering the quality and effects of food with such seriousness, as I had so many legitimate reasons to do so. But she also warned me to not ruminate. She pointed out that it only set me back to dwell on something, after-the-fact. I had heard this and even realized it myself many times before, but something about the way she pointed it out to me with love and authority made it stick.

We can only worry so much.

I felt so much validation being around her. We shared and enjoyed recipes together. We enjoyed exercising, sunshine, walks, and animals. It was wonderful.

THE MAN I'D BEEN talking to was from Illinois, within driving distance of my relatives in Michigan. He decided to come visit me in person for the first time. I asked that he only stay for one evening. I didn't want this trip to be about eHarmony contenders. This was something I needed down to the core. My relatives poured into me with love, encouragement, and acceptance.Brian arrived at the house with flowers. He was very polite and gentlemanly. We went to a park to walk around and chat, followed by a trip to Whole Foods—where I bought multiple flavors of Zevia, a stevia-sweetened soda I was addicted to.

The conversation went well. We discussed topics that would only be relevant for a committed relationship. He almost kissed me and said goodbye. He was off to pack for a trip to another country to visit his grandmother.

I PLAYED BASKETBALL WITH my cousins on Easter Day. I felt like me again! I was in *so* much pain the next day, but with no regrets. I went home with a heart full of hope and courage. I had a reason to stick around and keep trying. I had people who loved me and believed in me. I had momentum again. I had also successfully stuck to Carnivore for seven days, which was a new record. Every day I ate raw beef, raw beef liver, lightly cooked salmon, raw egg yolk, and bone marrow.

My cousins and I

On the last day of my trip, I broke code with keto ice creams. I stayed up extra late with my Uncle Rob while we sampled three different Halo Top flavors. They were all way too sweet. I had gotten my dopamine fix. I went to bed feeling no regret, because I didn't want to shut myself into a box. I didn't make myself sick. I had just had a successful trial run, and I was so prepared to carry on back home.

But I didn't have the same success when I got back. I quickly realized that where I was at here was not going to help me move forward. I had to change something. I couldn't stay in this same cycle. This environment was painful and limiting, almost suffocating.

I thought about this for the next few days. I had no more ties in this town. Even my own (immediate) family and I had little contact.

I spoke with Brian about the matter. I needed to be surrounded by others who could help me stay accountable to achieve my goals. I had such success in the few days I spent with my relatives—surely because it was a safe and supportive place, free from judgement, tension, and false accusations. I needed that.

The next half year was the most chaotic of my entire life.

So much so that I need to pause writing and come back in at least 48 hours.

1. Leptin:
https://www.webmd.com/diet/obesity/features/the-facts-on-leptin-faq
2. Orthorexia:
https://www.nationaleatingdisorders.org/learn/by-eating-disorder/other/orthorexia
3. Antinutrients:
https://www.sciencedirect.com/topics/food-science/antinutrients

11

Life with Brian

Early Spring, 2019

He proposed to me. Only because I made it very clear that marriage was my intention, and that I also needed someone to live with at this season of life. I was not doing well living on my own, and I also wanted to pursue the relationship.

I already know what you're thinking: *What an idiot!* And I wouldn't blame you. This was hands down the dumbest decision I had ever made. That decision was made from fear, though I told myself it was faith.

The *problem* was that I didn't have faith that God could heal me on my own. It was once again under the terms I felt best and most comfortable.

I wanted to try to skip the whole part where I had to fully depend on Him instead of myself or someone else.

TIP: This will never *work out.*

Though I was fully transparent about my struggles, it didn't justify the situation. I was not ready to be in any type of relationship whatsoever. Neither was he.

I STARTED PICKING UP on red flags during the big drive with the UHAUL. I started seeing a part of his personality I had not yet seen before. He was getting angry, irritable, and aggressive.

I was dealing with everything I had been dealing with for the past two years, but under a new type of pressure. I had to be strong now; not just for me, but for us. Somehow, I thought it would be better. The support I felt from my family at Easter was enough to make me believe that was the missing piece for me to stay consistent and slowly gain back my strength.

WHEN WE FINALLY ARRIVED at his house, my stomach dropped. He had told me he had a few things to clean up...

What I walked into was like a scene from the TV show "Hoarders."

Both sides of the sink were filled far over the top with piles of stacked dirty dishes, pans, cooking utensils. The countertops were also occupied by dirty dishes, half eaten things, and food items that were left out and not properly contained.

There were tools, PVC pipes, dirty rags, cement blocks, and a lot of other random things within eyesight from everywhere in the house. The room that I was to stay in had looked freshly slept in by another woman—undergarments lay on the bed and on the floor (apparently, they were from his mom who had recently stayed with him).

His yard was the only non-cluttered area, but I assumed this was due to him travelling heavily for the last 2-ish months.

It was a beautiful home, but it was beyond cluttered.

HE ALLOWED ME TO stay in the master bedroom with its own bathroom. I stayed up very late the night we arrived, unloading my meat into his freezer. He took all the junk food out of his cupboards, which I expected to not even exist. So much for Keto. For the record, eating avocados and eggs does not qualify as keto, so long as biscotti and popcorn are still in the equation. He also had copious amounts of fruit, rice, black pepper, and sauces full of sugar and MSG. I was bothered because earlier he had told me otherwise. I wouldn't have minded if he were forthright about these things from the get go. He threw everything into a bedroom and locked it up. I made it very clear before we came all the way out here that I could not have temptations within reach, as I was dealing with serious binge eating and food addiction. Later on, it did hurt me, by my own means.

I HAD TRIED THE Lion Diet at least eight times already and failed each time. Everyone in the Facebook support groups kept telling me to eat just beef, salt, and water! I felt worse each time.

Surely, I would get the same relief that I had when visiting with my aunt. Surely, I would start to get back up on my feet again. This was a new beginning.

THE NEXT DAY, I saw my new chiropractor, Doctor Ronald Rebbman.

I knew immediately that I could trust this man. He showed nothing but sincere concern for me. I received the best chiropractic adjustment of my life—this is not any exaggeration. I have a rib that slips regularly, and it's rare that someone can snap it into place without agitating it even more. I was so relieved!

He set me up with physical therapy paired with Graston, which was another great tool in recovering the effects of CREST Scleroderma. Layers and layers of scar tissue were broken up and muscles that I had never used before, nor known existed, were mobilized. This happened over the span of one year, with weekly appointments.

Systemic sclerosis (SS) is an autoimmune disorder. This means it's a condition in which the immune system attacks the body. Healthy tissue is destroyed because the immune system mistakenly thinks it's a foreign substance or infection. There are many kinds of autoimmune disorders that can affect different body systems.

Complications from scleroderma may be mild to severe and include:

Pitting or ulceration of fingertips due to reduced blood supply
Gangrene and amputation of fingertips in severe cases
Breathing difficulty due to scarring of lung tissue or pulmonary fibrosis
Pulmonary hypertension
Kidney problems, including increased levels of proteins in urine and renal failure
Scarring of heart tissues
Arrhythmias and congestive heart failure
Increased blood pressure

Dental decay
Constipation and/or diarrhea
Sexual dysfunction both in men and women[1]

Doctor Rebbman quickly became my accountability partner. He encouraged me to eat whole foods—real, unprocessed food. He listened and let me speak more than giving me any direction. He carefully considered and offered fantastic advice and guidance. He was honest about the things he didn't understand, and I liked that it didn't seem to bother him. He is confident in his strengths and uses them to serve and help others. He is the inspiration I needed at that time. He supported me in the ways that I clearly needed and encouraged me to do *what I knew was right.*

Back home, I was being accused of making up, or at least "playing on" all of my autoimmune disease, Lyme disease, and other illnesses. I was made to feel selfish for going to my chiropractor and taking walks every morning, and following everything that was in many ways my means to move forward. Routine is precious when you're at your wits' end with only a small capacity to function with every day.

Chronic disease can be so ugly and yet also invisible. Many times, you will not understand the amount of effort it takes for someone to simply get through a single day without falling apart completely. The Spoon Theory was brought to my attention by a dear friend who took to my side when I was diagnosed with Chronic Lyme. It resonated so much! Each day, I only had a limited number of spoons to give out. Once you understand this, you start you start to realize the importance of sticking to a routine.

Spoon theory is a metaphor that is used to describe the amount of mental or physical energy a person has available for daily activities and tasks. It was developed by Christine Miserandino in 2003 as a way to express how it felt to have lupus. She used spoons to provide a visual representation of units of energy that a person might have and how chronic illness forces her to plan out her days and actions in advance, so as not to run out of energy, or spoons, before the end of the day. It has since been applied to other phenomena, such as other disabilities, mental health issues, marginalization, and other factors that might place an extra—often unseen—burden on some individuals.

Getting up out of bed, putting on clothes, driving somewhere and eating, and having the strength to get back into bed and take a shower all in the span of a single day was like winning a medal at the Olympics. It was a grand occasion and something to be proud of. Washing hair was a luxury when it was difficult to hold up my own head. Everything—everything—felt like a struggle.

Now, you might be able to imagine how sticking to a routine could be so crucial. I felt it was my responsibility, because without it, I couldn't quite take care of myself. And if I couldn't take care of myself, how could I ever take care of others? It was conflicting in multiple ways.

AND SO, I LEFT one dynamic and entered into the worst yet...

The accusations turned into manipulation, shaming, betrayal, and verbal abuse.

I did not realize what narcissism was until I was warned by my massage therapist and friend from the local butcher shop.

---

1. Systemic Sclerosis: https://www.msdmanuals.com/home/bone,-joint,-and-muscle-disorders/autoimmune-disorders-of-connective-tissue/systemic-sclerosis

12

Epiphanies

May, 2019

My health continued to decline. My emotional state had never been worse. This was survival mode. I couldn't even bear to think about my family. I developed a calloused heart, because it was the only way to protect myself from so much pain.

"Just one day at a time," I told myself over and over, wishing it weren't so. I didn't want to be here anymore.

I came to the point of literally trying to get myself into residential eating disorder treatment. I had such a hard time re-feeding my body, and I was ready to pay someone to do it for me, even if it was with food that I wanted to avoid.

I ended up in an emergency room, needing to replenish electrolytes once again. They kept me for a couple of days. One of my dearest (and only) friends brought me my own food from the house, which was raw meat and bone marrow. I was released only to end back in another emergency room literally less than ten hours later. This time I had more of my preferred snacks that I was able to get delivered to my room from Instacart. Can you guess what I ordered?

Keto ice cream. I had also brought my stash of keto treats (mostly protein bars and peanut butter cups laden with chemicals and other nonsense). This stash wasn't organized anymore. This was my shameful stash, that I had previously requested to be locked away or hidden from me. I labeled these things in my mind as "not bad but not the worst", and that seemed fair. But when I honestly considered the relationship I had with these foods, I knew they *were* the worst—for me. I've never been tempted by candy or donuts; it's always been the keto or Paleo treats. I played games with myself for a long time, pretending that the addiction wasn't as bad if it were using less effective drugs.

I was dreadfully addicted. I felt gross. But I also felt like I needed these food items as a crutch. Because the "just beef, salt, and water" thing was ten times worse.

My ulcerative colitis (UC) had become so severe that I could not eat without involuntarily vomiting shortly after. I was *relieved* when the nurses witnessed this. I didn't want them to think I was making myself throw up. I was constantly depleted, puffy, and starving.

I was in constant fight/flight mode.

This is when I *asked* them to treat me with an eating disorder.

If I'm being completely honest, my number one goal was to get away from this toxic person. I would much rather have been safe at a hospital than at his home with him. I wanted so much to go back in time, again. This time I thought back to my treatment at UNC Chapel Hill—and I wanted to go back to there. At least my parents were concerned for me, and they were there when I got out. I remembered what it was like to fit into those yoga pants and I felt so broken and so far from ever being able to get to that place again.

I was fragile. I was 69 lbs at 5'6. I was stubborn. I was afraid. But I never gave up. I had hope that I couldn't identify quite yet.

I was sent to yet another emergency room that had an eating disorder program. I remember pulling up to this one, trying to find a parking spot, while on the phone with someone at a residential treatment center in another state that I was considering.

You see, I was at such a light weight that most residential treatment centers would not accept me. I needed to be treated in an acute setting.

I can't remember his name (I think it was Patrick), but I remember him asking me to pull over on the side of the road and do some breathing with him. He told me over and over it was gonna be OK and that I was gonna get away from this person. I was sobbing. I was a wreck. He probably saved me from getting *into* a wreck.

Thank God for his selfless spirit of generosity and kindness. He knew 1) my insurance didn't cover treatment with them, and 2) they wouldn't be able to host me if it did, due to my state of health. But that didn't make any difference to him in his decision to help me as best he could.

Sometimes, people really just need to see that someone is truly wanting and willing to help, even if they don't know what that looks like. It's just that sincerity and reassurance of "Yeah, you *are* worth it. You are loved. You will get through this. It's going to be okay. And it's *okay* to not be okay."

In my third consecutive emergency room, I openly shared that I was escaping domestic abuse. I wasted no time. I had no hesitations to lay it all out in the open. Why try to cover it up at this point?

They set me up in a room, and I can't be too sure, but I think that they purposely took their time with all the necessary procedures to keep me there as long as possible. I was in this room for an entire week.

The doctor wanted me to go into eating disorder treatment, but I couldn't with the C. Diff infection. I had to be held in isolation. All the doctors had to put on gowns, booties, masks, and gloves to even enter the room (I thought this was hilarious—my trashcan was always overflowing with their cover-ups).

I already knew the drill. I had berberine stashed in the room. That supplement always gave me relief, and it helped so much with blood sugar stabilization. I was dreading glucagon shots and hypoglycemia in this place—where it wouldn't be left untreated—and the method was not my favorite (*flashback UNC*).

I felt bad for being dishonest and hiding certain items. But I was still too stubborn to let them entirely take over. I also had my glucose and ketone monitor hidden in the room. I was taking blood sugar checks on top of theirs. It was unnecessary. It was false security. I just wanted to feel like I could do something about any of this.

As long as I had something to do, I felt like I was still in control...

Day after day, they sent up meals of 75% carbohydrates garnished with seed oils.

I continued to throw it away. All except for the meat and hard-boiled eggs. I tried to eat some of the salad with my own apple cider vinegar (yes, I did have my own apple cider vinegar as well). I was obnoxiously particular about what qualmed my stomach and regulated these symptoms that were nonstop and extremely intrusive. I was craving relief *all* the time.

I also had my yoga mat and resistance band with me in this room. I would do body weight squats, leg lifts, glute bridges, stretches, and Pilates. One time, the doctor walked in on me and yelled (literally) at me. She said I wasn't helping myself.

She was right, and that's when I stopped exercising. Exercise is therapeutic until it's abused, and then it's not. I had lost balance. I was surviving. I needed different coping methods.

As much as it helped calm my mind, it was working against my central nervous system. So, I focused on stretching and breathing. I also paced the 10-foot room.

One day, the dietician came to discuss options with me in my room. I actually recorded her repeating that it was 100% OK for me to eat an all-meat diet if it was helping me gain weight. I saved this recording to share with Brian so that he would stop harassing me. I had already gotten notes and permissions from my other doctors for him (at his demand), but none of it ever mattered. When they backed me up, he decided he didn't want those doctors or therapists to help me.

AT SOME POINT IN this 15-minute meeting, I let go of the fact that I would never be enough for Brian. I had to fend for myself. I had to make changes for myself, not for anyone else. I knew I would have to go back to him after my time here in the hospital. But I also knew it wouldn't be the same because I wasn't the same.

It's interesting how sometimes the greatest realizations arise simply when we're able to openly discuss a situation—without any goal but to get it out—and then our subconscious starts to connect dots and calculate what should stay and what should go.

Danny Vega of Fat Fueled Family was the first person to plant the seed of carnivore in my ear. I spoke with him over the phone a year prior, when I was going through tons of autoimmune issues. He said that the carnivore diet had been helpful for many. That was the first time I had ever heard of anti-nutrients in plant foods. I was unwilling to give up my avocados and baby spinach and so I didn't really consider his words until almost a year later, and that was when I first tried the carnivore diet. I tried it eight times by myself and failed each time because I found it to be too strict. But this time, it was different.

I told the dietician about the carnivore diet, and my journey so far. I told her I'd really thought there was something to it, but I had a really hard time sticking with it. I also told her I was willing to eat carbs if that's what I needed to do, but that they made me so sick and they only made the hypoglycemia worse.

That dietician put me in touch with the chef in the kitchen of the hospital. He started sending up entrees of meat, hard-boiled eggs, and butter multiple times per day.

I started hoarding and hiding these in my room. It wasn't perfect, and it was not a strict carnivore diet. But it made a difference almost immediately. My blood sugars stabilized. No longer did I need glucagon shots that would take my blood sugar from dangerous 30 mg/dl to the 200s in a matter of seconds.

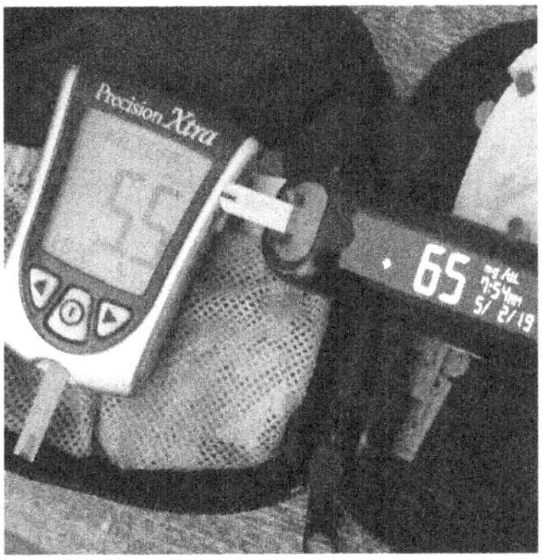

High-fat carnivore results

I will never forget the first time I survived a hypo without carbs or the shot. They encouraged me to eat an apple, and I asked them to let me eat meat instead. The really nice nurse was on staff that night; God was looking out. I sat there at 1:30 in the morning eating as much shredded pork as I could. For about two hours, I slowly ate it in silence. I didn't want the television or any lights on. I just sat there in the moonlight in my room, eating as much of this hospital meat as I could. I knew something big was happening. I could feel it in my spirit. I was excited. I was hopeful.

Sure enough, my blood sugar came back up in a very steady and slow fashion, stopping and maintaining at 85. There was no spike and/or plummet.

I continued to eat as much animal food as possible and within my one-week stay there, I had gained 4 lbs. No more involuntary throwing up. My electrolytes were all very stable.

What I wanted more than anything was my keto treats, but I knew I was done with them. It would be so foolish to even try. Filling up on meat made it so much easier to forget about. I had no physical desire for *any* of those treats anymore. Not in the least.

I had to surrender. I had to let go and let God in. I stopped taking the berberine, apple cider vinegar, and I stopped testing my own blood sugar. I was finally to the point that I was just too exhausted. This was my last chance. I had peace that humbled me and held me back from the urge to fight, almost like a weighted blanket.

God's grace lifted me up in that emergency room. I finally became so stable that I could no longer be held there as the doctor couldn't report anything to insurance. I had no legitimate reason to be held.

Her orders were to "*Go home and continue your weird all-meat diet.*"

AND THAT'S WHAT I did.

I felt major improvements in my mood and energy within the first two weeks.

This time was different. I was done wrestling with myself. I actually threw out my nasty stash of keto treats. I gave the ice cream away (I literally had at least 12 pints).

The Scripture-based affirmations that I had recited for so long finally started to come alive and manifest in my heart.

I understood that I belonged to Jesus. I am not my own. I literally cannot do anything without him. What he had done and was doing was undeniable.

I didn't care what carnivore support groups had to say. I didn't check. I didn't report anything to anyone. I sought God's will for my life, for the first time in my life, without any distractions.

I started taking cold showers, which seemed to help with mental resilience. I felt like I had a backbone again.

I didn't let Brian bully me anymore. His words didn't cut deep. In fact, I saw right through them. My brain started working better. My neurotransmitters were not shot, over saturated, or burnt out. They were firing better than ever.

On the mend

I started to believe what God said about me versus whatever anyone else had said about me, or all of the doubt that people had in me. I started believing in God's love despite how much I loathed myself. He was changing me. This was a real relationship, not religion. I was fully exposed, and I knew that I was loved.

All the failure and shame I identified with, God's grace lifted me out of it. His grace was sufficient.

Grace should not be confused with mercy. Grace is something that I never deserved, something that I couldn't ask for.

Mercy is being let off the hook for a crime. Grace is being blessed despite any crime.

And in order to receive a gift like God's grace, we have to acknowledge The Giver. Surrender will always be the word I use when people ask, "What was the most important lesson through all of this?" It is surrender.

By surrendering my own will and my need for control, I received wisdom. I started to use critical thinking skills instead of relying on a plan that would only make me worse.

Brian asked me to leave. I had to take steps before I knew which direction to go. One day at a time.

I called everyone on my contacts list for help with a place to live.

I called multiple shelters in my area, and they were full for the season.

I started knocking on my neighbors' doors during my walks.

One was a believer. She prayed with me and she did all she could to get through to these shelters to get me in.

She bought me a Costco membership to help with gas money.

It was so encouraging to just have someone care and try to help, even if she couldn't offer any solution. She really did try. She let me into her home to check in over the next couple of weeks and treated me like a normal human being.

13

Spiritual Warfare

THE MORE MY EYES opened up to how poorly I was being treated, the more motivated I was to get out. I realized that God wanted so much more for me. I settled for something so far from what He desired, and I wouldn't find peace in this situation even if I tried. That would take a combined effort.

Sure, I was 73 lbs and still very frail, but I had momentum now. I didn't know how it was going to work out, but I knew that it would. God wouldn't have spoken to me in such a clear way in the hospital room for me to not escape this situation. He gave me that confirmation and I had a sureness and stillness in my spirit. It was His spirit.

Everything I had heard from others—in sermons, admired in others, read in the Bible, or even sung about in songs—and everything that struck a chord with me and stayed with me about God and who He really is, started to become real. It was more than just something I believed—it was something I lived by, breathed by. It became the reason I got out of bed. I had a reason to be consistent, and to focus on the positives. I was operating from Faith, and no longer fear. I had been set free, even though I was still suffering. It was a lot, but not overwhelming. I found the love I was created for and longed for my whole life.

HE ALWAYS MAKES A way. It was getting easier for me to depend on and rest in His promises. Even as I was being harassed and battered around, I found rest and kept my peace. I started getting deeper sleep and waking up without dread. This was a radical and unforgettable shift.

ONE DAY, MY PHONE broke as I was cleaning up the kitchen. This had been my fourth replacement in less than two months. I am a class A klutz, but I had no doubt that this was spiritual warfare. Never a shattered screen or water in a port—nothing I could pinpoint to cause a total shutdown of four consecutive replacements. Of course, the enemy noticed my hope. I had been trying to schedule an appointment with a Christian counselor and was finally ready to get together with her that evening.

I asked Brian if I could use his phone to call for another replacement.

He started laughing at me. Right there, with him standing in front of me, I realized just how desperate I had gotten. How far I had let this go that I could have been so blind to end up with this person who was seemingly heartless. I blurted out two words that I now regret (not worth repeating, but you might be able to guess). My blood was boiling.

He caught on that I was no longer taking his crap to heart, let alone tolerating it. I was standing up to him every day now.

One day, I threatened to call the police if he didn't stop harassing. I followed through, and they shared with me that even if he wanted to evict me, I would still have a full 30 days before the process could even begin—and then *he* would be the one having to leave first, considering the circumstances.

I had already spoken with most of the police department in this town. They all knew what I was dealing with and would check in when they saw me out on one of my walks. A couple of times, I met with a particular officer late at night at a rec center across the street. He wanted to maintain in-person updates. I appreciated that, even though they could not help with the potential of being homeless.

View of Brian's house on one of my walks

They knew who Brian was before I even provided an exact address. Most of the neighbors knew who he was. He was "the guy that didn't pay any attention to the Home Owners Association (HOA) rules". He always kept his curtains closed. His front yard was overgrown.

Brian had (or has) good qualities, but his attitude and behaviors were always inconsistent. I received warnings from his closer friends shortly after I had moved there.

NOW THAT IT WAS very obvious this relationship was going nowhere, he decided to start charging me rent. He moved me into the smaller bedroom and asked me to pay him through his new Airbnb listing.

One of his friends came over to "help move my stuff into the new room".

I had never in my life met such a desperately broken and cruel person as this woman.

She didn't even know who I was. She only knew what he had told her about me.

"You must be a really horrible person for your own parents to kick you out and abandon you."

The cruel comments continued all night. She accused me of damaging his countertop with my air fryer and demanded that he get pictures so that they could sue. I kept moving and kept my mouth shut.

It didn't hurt me. I felt bad for her. It was like grade school. I could see why the two of them got along.

At one point, he told me there was nothing else I could do and suggested I go take a walk. I think even he was tiring of her obnoxious behavior.

I went outside to my car and started crying. I called a prayer friend, and we started to rebuke the enemy.

This woman marches out the front door to my car and starts banging on my window.

"How dare you come out here and sit in your car while we do all the work!" She barked.

"He told me there was nothing else I could do," I replied.

"You better come out here and help. Come out here right now. *Right now!*" She was like a toddler throwing a fit.

Still on the other phone line, my friends were continuing to pray and encouraged me to not falter. "Don't respond. Don't respond, Rebekah."

"Thanks, I have to go."

"Okay Rebekah, stay strong and we are praying for you."

Proverbs 27:17 says, "Iron sharpens iron, and one man sharpens another." When iron blades are rubbed together, each becomes sharper and thus more effective. Likewise, when believers are involved in one another's lives, mutual edification occurs.

THAT NIGHT I WAS so exhausted. I locked the bedroom door, lay down in bed, and installed the Airbnb app to pay for the room.

"I've sent so many messages. What's a few more?" I thought.

I must have sent out around 18 or so messages in the next 40 minutes. It was a brief explanation of my circumstances and a blatant request for *help*. I needed a safe place to stay so that I could get back on my feet.

I had reached out to many people online already. I received a lot of responses, especially from people on Craigslist. But at the last minute, they would always let me know that there was a catch. It usually involved something inappropriate and offensive. It was disheartening how much I ran into this.

A lot of people did respond with encouraging words, but unfortunately did not have the means to help me. After three out-of-pocket fecal transplants and a lifelong list of medical treatments and supplements, not to mention an inability to work, I did not have much to offer. I could babysit, I could cook and clean. I could try to work, but it wouldn't be enough.

I was ready for a miracle. I knew I was already walking in one. So, I prayed for another. I boldly asked God for a new, safe place to live. I asked him out loud, in the dark, on my bed, with my phone in my hands and hot tears on my face.

And that's what I got.

14

Saving Grace

A COUPLE OF HOURS passed while most messages received replies. I was about to unplug for the night when I received one more, right around midnight.

This host replied saying they would be willing to offer me a space for free, with nothing in return.

I didn't get my hopes up. I was prepared for a catch. We exchanged phone numbers, and I went to sleep.

He texted me shortly after I woke up the next morning with a link to the listing that he had a room for me at. He told me he would help me long term, and that he wanted to help. I asked him if there was any catch, and he assured me there wasn't. He described a parable of Jesus and a beggar. "And I couldn't help but think about how I'm out here grinding, doing the best I can with the blessings I've been given. How could I not use those same blessings to bless someone who needs it and yes haha sorry for the story."

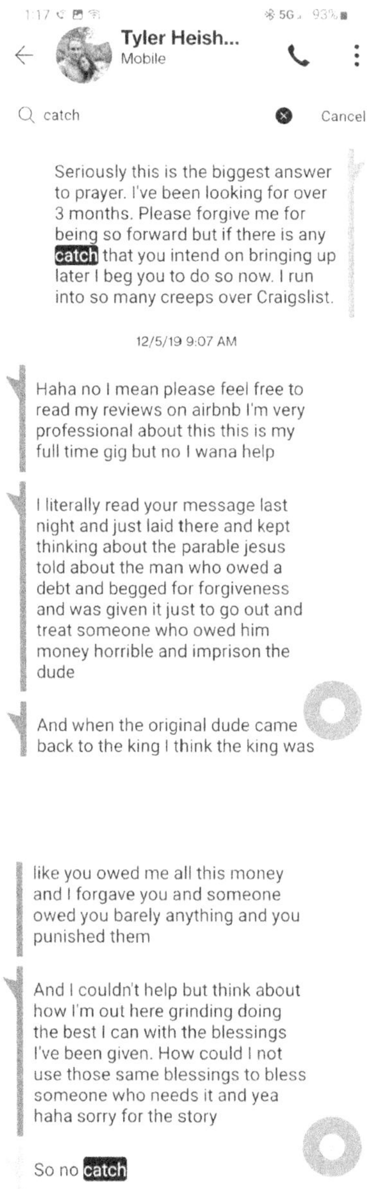

Talking to him felt familiar.

That same evening, I visited the place that was offered by this kind stranger. As I arrived at my destination via Google Maps, my heart nearly skipped five beats.

As I sat in his dirt driveway, I noticed that directly to my left was the shelter I had delivered a turkey dinner to with my butcher friend just the month before. The same shelter I reached out to a couple of weeks after that only to have them tell me they had no space. It was so run down.

His home was in the ghetto. I could have cared less about that.

I will never forget the first time I met Tyler.

The door was swung open by a tall, handsome, friendly stranger in a bright pink Polaroid hoodie.

Is this man gay? I thought to myself as I noticed his perfect eyebrows. *Nah, he just has great eyebrows.*

We walked up a particularly steep flight of stairs in the very back of the house to the upstairs bonus room. At the very back was a nice sized room with a single window facing the front of the house. There was no heat in this room, and it had quite a draft. I loved it more than I could put into words. There was nothing special about this room. But at that moment, I felt very safe. And in the next moment, Tyler asked if he could give me a hug. I was safe.

He introduced me to his beautiful husky puppy named Milky Way. I smiled the entire way home.

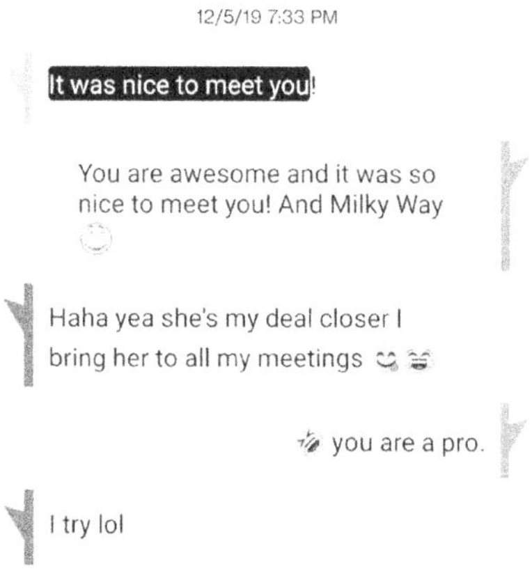

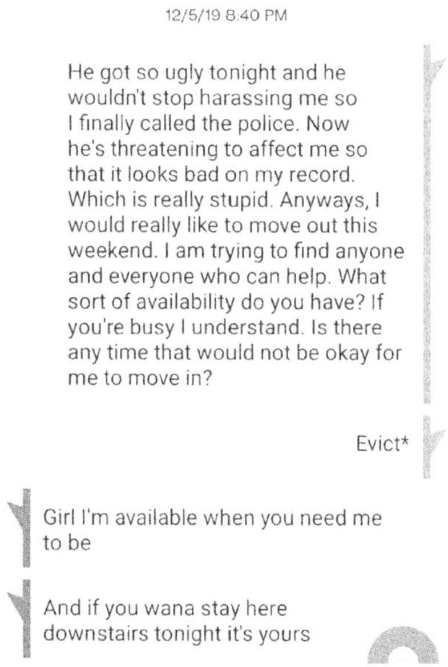

I moved in three days later.

My butcher friend and her brother were there to help, along with one of the neighbors. Tyler showed up with his Charger and pink Polaroid hoodie at Brian's house to help. I felt very happy and grateful. My junk filled his entire basement. And even more of my things were stacked from floor to ceiling in his living room, his kitchen, and my new bedroom. He didn't seem stressed at all. He told me to finally sleep well now that I was in a safe place.

THIS NEW HOUSE HAD six bedrooms and one bathroom. I had used the bathroom in empty pizza boxes behind the trash can in the middle of the night multiple times. I also slipped in the snow doing so, multiple times.

Tyler allowed me to use his kitchen for my air fryer, crock pot, and food dehydrator. He never once made me feel insecure or ashamed for all the space I took up—he allowed me to just be there, and to be comfortable. He even had things like plastic wrap for me to use. He never asked for anything in return. This was an environment I could grow in. I had space. And even though he hadn't vocalized it (yet), I knew that he truly believed in me. It gave me courage, before I even recognized that's what he had done for me. Even as I write this, I am still realizing new ways to be so grateful for Tyler. He continues to be one of the greatest blessings in my life.

Each morning I made the same breakfast, which was a variety of animal foods. I ate a lot of fish skins at this time—air fried into crispy chips. This is something I came up with mostly due to being very broke and craving something crispy and salty. Chances are, your local seafood merchant would be willing to set aside their fish skins for you to scale, cut into squares, and crisp up. The only problem: They're fishy. They smell *very* fishy. So fishy that I eventually was asked to move my air fryer up to the bonus room because the smell was too much.

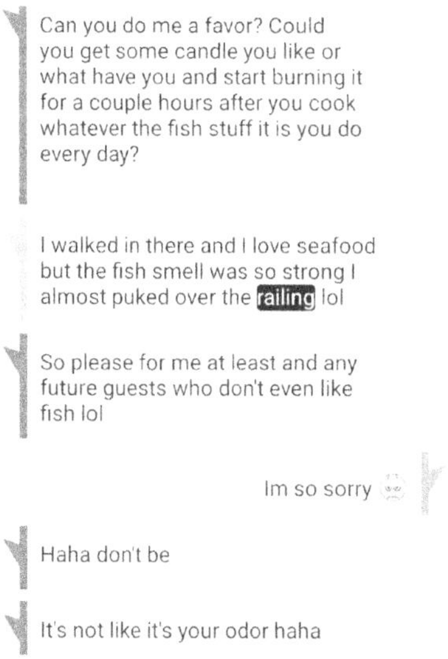

I was slightly embarrassed. I was so focused on fueling my starving body that I didn't concern myself with these things. Now, the smell is overwhelming to me. God delivered me of the fish skins over a year ago now (hahaha). They accounted for half of my protein at first. Protein is expensive. But so is being too malnourished to live life.

I continued to trek up and down the steep stairs multiple times every morning to load the air fryer, toss the fish skins twice, and wash the air fryer. Sometimes self care involves hard work. It's worth it. You're worth it. I was excited to have the energy to go up and down those stairs multiple times, just to eat.

I sat down at the dining room table with my Scriptural Affirmations by Charles Capps.

I loved taking walks before breakfast. I loved coming back home to a place that I could relax. I did not have anxiety about coming home, and that was a gift.

I had zero cravings aside from Zevia.

I had no impulses to binge.

THERE WERE TWO GUESTS who were staying long term when I first moved in. They were getting into fights fairly frequently, and I'm pretty sure they were on drugs a couple of times.

I still felt safe as long as Tyler knew. I knew that he was going through his own stuff, but he always took care of things for everyone else.

I made friends with everyone who came there to stay.

It was so wonderful to meet people who didn't already have some horrible impression of who I was.

One guest decided to quit his vegan diet after living with me for a couple of weeks.

I WILL NEVER FORGET that house. It was the beginning of very deep healing physically, emotionally, and even spiritually. Late in the evening I would come downstairs to sit in my recliner chair with my legs up the wall, and read out of Psalms and Proverbs. There was just enough light to read coming from a nightlight.

I could hear the couple from one of the bedrooms talking and laughing while they played video games. They would stay up all night, almost every night, and ate nothing but pizza, hot dogs, and macaroni. Later on, I realized they had limited options due to not having a car and shopping at the Dollar General around the corner.

The girl was from Germany and was visiting the States to be with the boy. They were both so sweet. She became a lifelong friend and though we don't talk often, the conversations we've had will seal a bond for a lifetime. There were a handful of heart-to-heart conversations in that home.

God places people in our lives so strategically.

15

A New Chapter of Healing

My sleep improved, and my digestion improved to some degree. My mood continued to improve, as well as my energy.

Though I knew I was not in immediate danger, I still felt the effects of trauma pulsing through my body, mind, and spirit. I didn't feel irritable or agitated like I used to, but I still felt far from rested.

On the coldest winter days, I would still wear shorts out on my morning walk before breakfast. I was numb from the inside out, but I was on the mend. I knew that healing from trauma was a process, so I gave myself grace. I learned that it was OK to not be OK. So long as I continued to seek God and His will first, I knew I would be alright.

I still felt a lot of physical pain, and I think part of that is almost inevitable at a certain level of malnourishment. I was much more resilient and had an overall greater capacity, but that also meant my body was working harder.

I did yoga every evening (just stretching and breathwork). I loved how cushioned my body felt with my extra cushioned yoga mat on top of the carpet. It helped me to remember to breathe deeply. It helped me to remember to engage my core, stretch, and move with mindfulness. It was a reminder that I had made it through another day of *healing*. I was soaking up all the gratitude and comfort.

ONE DAY, TYLER TEXTED to give me a heads up that there would be a long-term stay at the Airbnb.

That night I woke up to some really loud noises downstairs. Gabby had arrived hot and bothered, fresh out of Texas with all of her belongings packed like sardines into her Camry (which was blocking my car in the driveway).

She talked at a quicker pace than I was used to. I instantly felt overwhelmed and overly stimulated. I almost felt defensive of this quiet, safe place that had become my haven. But I knew I couldn't take any such stance. I also knew that I was extra sensitive. I asked God to help me be patient, kind, and loving.

The next day, her boyfriend came over to visit. I tried my best to cover the very loud, intimate noises coming from the bedroom while I was preparing my dinner. *Now* I was irritated. I continued to press in and ask God to help me. I had no right to be such a stick in the mud.

I never would have imagined the friendship that blossomed between us.

With each and every conversation something seemed to strike my heart. She was authentic and sometimes a hot mess. She Facetimed her mom on the phone a lot and not only told me about her pets, her life in Texas, her job hunt, and everything in between. She voluntarily immersed me into it all. She was *real*, and I loved that.

She started joining me for after dinner walks and even pre-bedtime yoga. Sometimes—*many* times—we would just end up in Baby pose, laughing like idiots. I felt like I could really let loose and be dorky old me with her. It reminded me of the friendship I had before I got sick—the one that fell apart because I got sick and couldn't be around anymore. I had felt misunderstood. My friendship with Gabby reminded me of the importance of being known. It really is that simple and yet such a rare treasure.

We made snow angels together during the first snowfall that season. It was her first snow ever, and the first time I had enjoyed real snow since I was a child.

Gabby was one of my first official clients!

Gabby was my second official client as a certified Health and Life Coach. My first had been back in 2017, shortly after I was diagnosed with chronic Lyme disease and I moved back in with my parents.

Back in 2017, I was pursuing disability. God put it on my heart to become a health coach. I made cards and started sharing to my Instagram. I had my first client, Alyssa, back then. But I had to put that on the back burner for a little while. Around the time I was held in the eating disorder unit against my will, the dynamic at home was so toxic that I didn't really have the mental space to progress as a health coach. But God was surely preparing me through everything that I went through up until 2020. When I moved into Tyler's bonus room, I earned my certifications through the Health Coach Institute and Gabby became my client during that time.

In a matter of weeks, she lost a significant amount of weight, and her mood and energy improved. Her relationship with food had changed dramatically. Her self-esteem and confidence were the biggest changes that I recognized.

She ended up dumping her boyfriend and moving back to Texas, going to school, and meeting someone new. She actually just posted some beautiful engagement photos.

There couldn't have been anyone more appropriate to be a part of my life during that time.

God is so intentional with whom he places in our lives.

I REACHED OUT TO a couple of local farmers to establish relationships with. I think this is a smart thing to do for anyone eating meat more than 3x per week. Why *not* cut out the middleman and support hard-working people who take care of our animals and our land?

www.eatwild.com is a great resource for anyone looking to source local farmers.

One particular company has been a greater blessing to me than what I could ever put into words.

Billy Doe Meats responded promptly when I reached out. They sent me a variety of cuts just to try! These people loved, encouraged, and supported me every single step of the way. We are now family. This is the meat that I healed eating. But also, these are the people who believed in me when I was still very broken. They came alongside me and showed me true kindness. They offered me the gift of authentic friendship. Hoda and I still chat on a regular basis. She calls to simply say hello, or to check in. She is comfortable sharing the harder things with me, and vice versa. Our friendship has been built and thrives on love. The Billy Doe Meats family will always hold a special place in my heart. I'm thrilled to share them with others who find total breakthroughs when they try non-aged, holistically raised meat for the first time. The quality is outstanding and unmatched.

I found support systems in places that I never would have imagined.

My friend Libor, the only 100% carnivore that I knew in real life back in 2020

The gym, my chiropractor, the grocery store. People do care. And for as many people that will hurt you and leave you for dead, there are still those who will love you to no end. Now I understand that this comes from the Father. He cares for us, and he looks out for us. We are responsible to receive these blessings, and to walk in His will, even when isolation might be more comfortable. I receive when I ask, reach out, and step out. It's important to prepare and literally posture ourselves to receive the things we're praying for—otherwise, are you believing for it in Faith?

MY STRUCTURED, DAILY ROUTINE helped me deal with the stress that I still felt about my family and financial issues. I continued to get stronger and feel better.

Then one day, Tyler asked myself and Gabby to leave. I was crushed, but I also understood. I was anxious about what I would do, but not afraid. This was part of the process. God had me, and I was actively trusting His promises. Disappointment couldn't even begin to threaten me like it did before. Now, it was more like news to observe, without judgement or any emotional engagement. God was going to continue to provide. I *knew* this now.

> *"For I know the plans I have for you, declares the Lord, plans for welfare and not for evil, to give you a future and a hope."*
>
> *—Jeremiah 29:11*

I set out again looking for roommates. I couldn't afford very much per month, with disability alone and some help from a dear friend on occasion to help pay for food.

Let's just say I wouldn't have voluntarily eaten so many fish skins every day if they hadn't been a free source of protein. I cut corners in any and every way that I felt I could.

I found a couple of potential roommates who were (initially) cool with me paying the lesser amount that I could offer, until I had more to offer. I spent weeks looking for a place with them, scheduling and touring, trying to coordinate. I was the one who started the whole process and I introduced them to each other.

The week that I had to move out, they decided to get their own place together, unless I could agree to different terms. They backed me up against the wall in a way that they probably knew I couldn't comply. It was cruel.

As much as I wanted to make promises to pay more by a specific date, I couldn't. I understood their stance, but I did not understand their actions.

I've never understood the act of leading someone on. What good does it do for anyone? Deep in my heart I knew they weren't the right people to live with anyways. So, it goes—and God was still providing.

That same evening, I met with one other person who was also looking for a roommate, whom I had met on Facebook Marketplace.

TJ was sweet and timid. We took a short walk and decided to meet again to find a place.

We were going to sign an apartment lease together at some super affordable apartments down the street. TJ message me the day I was supposed to have found my own place. He had lost his job due to the pandemic, and could not move forward. He was extremely apologetic, and I knew that he was sincere in his apologies.

In a moment, I knew what I had to do—without a shadow of a doubt. I was standing up from the couch in the dining room (yes, it was my small couch, crammed into the dining room because Tyler's house was still filled with my junk), and I had a certain confidence that this was going to work. I called the landlord of a four-unit condo that I saw by myself the week prior when I was still looking for the (original plan) three of us. It wasn't something that I could afford by myself, but I couldn't forget it. I felt right at home. Maybe it was the charm of original hardwood floors, doors, kitchen cupboards, and doorknobs, or the fact that it was tiny but also had large closets, lots of counterspace, and a massive window that flooded the living room with sunlight.

I got in touch with my family for the first time in about 6 months. I explained everything that had happened, and that I was getting better, slowly but surely. My dad lovingly, cautiously agreed to be the co-signer.

It wasn't a lengthy or drawn-out conversation of shaming or pointing fingers or anything like that. I've always appreciated this about my dad—he forgives and he believes in me, even when he still has reason to doubt. My dad has always encouraged me in the best ways.

My plan was to rent out the two extra bedrooms so I could afford to live there. It was a leap of Faith. Simon, my new landlord, could not have been sweeter or more understanding.

His wife, Julie, spoke to me on the phone and told me that I was the person they had been praying for, for years. I believe it. They were who I was praying for!

I moved in with the help of friends from the gym. This was the last day I had available to use a UHAUL—as even they were closing down for the pandemic. God made a way when there seemed to be none.

Only a couple of weeks later, TJ texted me again. He got his job back, and so he ended up moving in. We found another cool roommate within a couple of months.

I GAINED 65 HEALTHY pounds in one year.

I reversed hypothyroidism (twice), every single autoimmune disease (over ten), chronic Lyme disease, and chronic Clostridium Difficile.

My labs are "textbook perfect", aside from extremely high B12 which is not a problem especially as someone with the MTHFR genetic mutation.

> ***"The MTHFR gene mutation links to a decreased ability to detoxify, as well as over 60 chronic health conditions including Hashimoto's and hypothyroidism, blood clots, infertility, cardiovascular disease, Alzheimer's, depression, birth defects, and certain cancers."***[1]

I was living proof that the "uncurable" was curable, that there was nothing truly irreversible. Epigenetics is real, powerful, and practical. By modifying nutrition and lifestyle, we are able to change the way that our genes express themselves.

> ***epigenetics***
> ***[ˌepəjəˈnediks]***
> ***NOUN***
> ***biology***
> ***the study of changes in organisms caused by modification of gene expression rather than alteration of the genetic code itself.***[2]

I DID NOT EXPECT health coaching to be enough to carry me financially. I had never been able to do so in my entire life.

But God is just so good like that. He *exceeds* our greatest expectations. He already knew how much I could handle and how he would provide. He has been waiting my entire life for me to surrender to him, depend on him, and abide in him—so that I can experience the richness, sweet joy, and abundance of His love and kindness.

God brings good people into our lives and gives us strength when we need it the most!

When I first started health coaching, I couldn't imagine working with more than four people at one time, especially being an "unlimited" health and life coach—available at all times.

Today I am working with twenty-eight clients, and I still have time to be in bed by 8:00 p.m. I function mostly in a "flow state"—no more "fight and flight" mode. Productivity is not a question of possibility. I have motivation, energy, and peace even under stress. Things don't get under my skin like they used to.

I wake up with wonderful energy and rarely any pain. I have focus like never before. I do CrossFit six days per week. I look forward to cleaning my small condo instead of having to strategically plan for it with the tiny capacity or stamina I had before. I look forward to working with and walking alongside others. I am so blessed! Faith changes everything. I am healed physically, but also spiritually. My heart posture has changed, and that changes my experience. I look forward to what is ahead and forget what is behind (while holding onto the lessons I've learned along the way).

I'm writing this book now because I *get* to. I am responding to the call. I get to share this amazing message of hope. I get to walk alongside others as they go through their own healing journeys. And I will continue to do so for as long as God so provides or until He calls me elsewhere.

I want to be clear that my situation did not turn to butterflies and rainbows overnight.

Renewing my mind with God's Word—the Truth—changed my perspective and my belief system. It gave me strength, purpose, and vision. Without those things, I would not be who I am, or where I am. Without Jesus I would not be here.

Gratitude practice pulled me in the right direction, whereas negativity and discouragement only ever weighed me down and stole my joy and peace.

---

1. The MTHFR Gene Mutation: https://www.healthline.com/health/mthfr-gene

2. Epigenetics: https://medlineplus.gov/genetics/understanding/howgeneswork/epigenome/

16

In My Element

Fall, 2021

THE WEEK BEFORE I write this, I had hosted the very first Tailored Keto Health Retreat in the Smoky Mountains.

I had the opportunity to spend every day surrounded by God's creation with amazing, like-minded people. On the second day, Tyler joined me outside on the patio in a moment of silence as I took in the beautiful day and all of its blessings.

"You're beautiful. You're definitely in your element."

I was in my element. I am doing what God is calling me to. I am pouring out and opening up my heart the in the way God fashioned it for.

I can't quite describe the joy it brings to share some of my on-the-fly recipes with others who are looking for a way to make this way-of-eating sustainable. Who wouldn't want to use food as medicine? Who wouldn't want to have their cake and eat it too? I made this way of eating work because *I had to*. But thankfully, many people don't take it that far, and could really benefit from the various techniques, tips, and tricks I've discovered along the way.

Who wouldn't want to have food freedom and optimal health?

This is a lifestyle. This is not a diet. This is honoring my body and taking care of it, so that I can be who God created me to be.

This is not restriction. This is the first time I've been free from addiction, unhealthy cycles and patterns, and crutches.

Last week Tyler asked me to be his girlfriend (10-27-2021). Now we go to CrossFit together every day. *I couldn't be happier or more grateful*. A year ago, I was praying for him to find Jesus. I never thought he would be in my life again, and that was hard for me to accept for a while. Now, I honestly can't quite imagine my life without him. I love Tyler with all of my heart. I know the Lord has a bright future in store for both of us. I am so grateful for this present moment. I find myself no longer longing for a future I can only dream of, or a past I try to patch together in the most delightfully-memorable way... I want for nothing. I am just so grateful and excited. I am eager to share this hope with others.

And when things fall apart in life, as they always do, I know that I will still be filled with joy and an eternal hope. This eternal hope is an anchor for my soul. I know that I will still have my tribe—these people God brings into our lives. It is no coincidence, and it's not "the universe aligning". No, it's the love of your Abba, Father, reaching out to you even if you're too lost or frightened to recognize that.

Jesus Christ never changes. Jesus is the reason for healing. Meat is the medicine and God is the healer.

We have victory and abundance in Christ. The battle has been won.

If you never discover this truth, you will live under a false guise of defeat. The devil knows this and will do *all* that he can to keep you from discovering your true identity.

> *"As a man thinketh in his heart, so is he."*
>
> —Proverbs 23:7

> *"So now there is no condemnation for those who belong to Christ Jesus."*
>
> —Romans 8:1

My mom and I at the beach together

I TALK WITH MY mom almost every day. We talk about things that I've never felt comfortable talking to her about before. It's not just that I'm an adult now, or the dynamic of no longer living together. There is a new established bond of trust, respect, and understanding because we made it through to the other side together. Though she could not meet me where I was once at, she loved me through it the best she knew how. I couldn't fathom how her actions could be called love. But now, putting myself in her shoes, I understand. If my own flesh and blood were wasting away before my eyes, I might do something a little rash for the sake of saving them. She has also confided in me, through various conversations on what happened, that they had advised to cut me off. I've never received specifics and I don't ever plan on asking. Nobody needs to revisit that painful time.

My mom is my best friend. We have conversations about everything, and nothing. We sometimes just stay on the phone together, in silence.

Our relationship is so much better now

Once upon a time, she might have frowned upon my remarks of antinutrients or the benefits of extended fasting and beef liver. Now, she's calling me to ask how to use beef bones for homemade broth, and which electrolytes are best.Helping family is something else—it's always different than helping others. It's almost like the advice has to come from somewhere else other than yourself to be received, considered, or even acknowledged. Sometimes I wish I could disguise myself as a neighbor to drop pieces of health advice to my parents and sister. Sometimes that sort of information is better received by someone on the outside—someone not related. Perhaps it's pride, or perhaps it's just too close for comfort. Whatever it may be, respect and boundaries should be maintained. Too much force is not ever excused by pure or well-intended motives. I believe that tough love is *letting* someone learn the hard way, not *forcing* them to. It's loving them despite their weaknesses and hoping the best for them as well as supporting them despite the same continuous repeated mistakes they may have made or are still making. Love always hopes, trusts, and perseveres. But Love does not force itself upon anyone.

"*There is no fear in love, but perfect love casts out fear.*"
—John 4:18

My mom reminds me of things that shouldn't, but do slip from my conscious awareness. She has reminded me that I too really was in an even worse place than what some of my clients are going through right now. This is why I have the capacity to understand and walk alongside them. I'm able to act as a buoy out in the sea (to use my friend Lisa's analogy). I've already lost sight of the shore, and even when you may be afraid to swim, I will be here to remind you that it's going to be okay. It has been done. Letting go and trusting is the only way. My mom and I pray for my clients together and though she does not get all of the details, she writes down their names.

"I can only imagine, Mom…what they have gone through to get to this point."

"You don't have to imagine; you yourself were there. You were that lost. You had lost your mind. And that's why you can help them now."

I did once lose my mind. I lost hope, and the will to live. I lost sight of my purpose, all purpose. I pray every day for the Lord to never let me forget just how far he has brought me. I was so numb for so long. I couldn't hear my own thoughts or control them. I couldn't calm down the rattling raging train inside. I was exhausted, but never finding rest.

Part 2

My Faith Journey

17

The Power of Prayer

THESE PAST COUPLE OF years I've only just begun to really understand the power of prayer. The devil wants to keep us distracted, doubting and putting our prayer lives on the back burner, because he knows how powerful it is. He knows that when we start to commune with our Creator, all fear will dissipate in the power of His Love.

My prayer life does not just look like quiet time first thing in the morning. It looks like turning on worship music when I feel like being frustrated. It looks like talking to God in the grocery store, or out on a walk, simply admiring his creation.

Prayer can also look like crying on my knees with a heart posture of gratitude, yet still a deep longing to grow closer to Him... because he is the sweetest thing I've ever known.

Sometimes it's just listening, and intentional silence.

There was a study conducted on those who lived through the Holocaust. First, the survivors were asked to think about the worst thing they ever experienced. Blood pressures did not rise, nor did cortisol levels.

Then the same participants were asked to speak about the worst thing they ever experienced. Some had elevated blood pressure levels to the point of near heart attacks.

The power of the spoken word is not appropriately known, appreciated, or utilized!

If you want to change the way that you think as well as your actual—physiological—self, use your words.

You don't have to believe it before you claim it. If you say something out loud enough times, you will start to believe it and it will become true for you. You can use this for good or for bad.

In 2017, I met with a mentor from my Church during the week. I was so broken up inside and I just needed help. I don't think I knew what that help could be at the time, but I didn't have any good relationship with my immediate family to confide in or reach out to them. Most of my friendships had also suffered to the point of non-existence. The friends that stayed still didn't understand. This was nobody's fault, just a fact.I spoke of the autoimmune crisis I was facing, and the fact that I kept losing weight and my family thought I had an eating disorder. I was seemingly stuck—caught in between a rock and a hard place. I didn't expect the response I did receive.He asked if I had been reading my Bible—"Because the way you're talking tells me you aren't!"

It was exactly what I needed to hear, and also not anything I wanted to hear. He gave me my first Scriptural Affirmations book by Charles Capps. I took it home and learned the lesson that I hope I've imparted in this short chapter. In this book, I was instructed to recite God's promises of healing and hope over my life, out loud, three times per day until Faith grows and then once per day for maintenance. I felt so silly reading those instructions, but deep down I knew it was going to challenge and humble me.

If I had true Faith, none of it would have seemed silly or felt awkward.

I had been using words and verbiage that dignified the disease and sickness in my body more than words of Hope or Faith or the abundant life waiting for me only when my heart was ready to surrender and receive.

Much later on, I decided to stop speaking of anything negative unless it was necessary. Instead of saying "my Chronic Lyme" or "my chronic pain", I would instead refer to it as nothing but a symptom, separate from me. It's so easy to let these things define us. It is almost encouraged in some situations to "embrace" these ailments—especially the "uncurable" ones—because even health professionals know and are sensitive to the fact that unrealistic expectations are the source of great disappointment. Why get anyone's hopes up when it all seems so bleak? I can understand all of this coming from someone who doesn't know Jesus Christ. But for a Believer, I think this is dangerous and toxic.

The Lord wants to exceed your expectations. He also promises to be your source of comfort, joy, peace, and strength during the most difficult and trying times.

Don't just hold on to His promises. Surrender to them as the whole Truth that they are. Claim them.

> "*The tongue can bring death or life; those who love to talk will reap the consequences.*"
>
> —Proverbs 18:22

Indeed, we all make many mistakes. For if we could control our tongues, we would be perfect and could also control ourselves in every other way.

We can make a large horse go wherever we want by means of a small bit in its mouth. And a small rudder makes a huge ship turn wherever the pilot chooses to go, even though the winds are strong. In the same way, the tongue is a small thing that makes grand speeches.

But a tiny spark can set a great forest on fire. And among all the parts of the body, the tongue is a flame of fire. It is a whole world of wickedness, corrupting your entire body. It can set your whole life on fire, for it is set on fire by hell itself.

People can tame all kinds of animals, birds, reptiles, and fish, but no one can tame the tongue. It is restless and evil, full of deadly poison. Sometimes it praises our Lord and Father, and sometimes it curses those who have been made in the image of God. And so blessing and cursing come pouring out of the same mouth.

"Surely, my brothers and sisters, this is not right! Does a spring of water bubble out with both fresh water and bitter water? Does a fig tree produce olives, or a grapevine produce figs? No, and you can't draw fresh water from a salty spring."

—James 3:2-12

18

God: The Healer

I USED TO DREAD the morning. I used to dread waking up to the nightmarish reality. My body would ache at such a deep level that I would feel nauseous. My bones ached. The fear that ruled me would make me so disgustingly discontent. I got up every single day was because of God's promise that his mercies are new every morning. I also felt more pain doing nothing than doing something. Nothing feels worse than giving up when you know you shouldn't.

> *"The steadfast love of the Lord never ceases; his mercies never come to an end; they are new every morning; great is your faithfulness."*
>
> *—Lamentations 3:22-23*

Maybe today would be different. Maybe today I would stand up to the impulse to binge on seemingly helpful foods with a behavior that brought death to my spirit. Maybe today I would reach some level of understanding with my own family. I didn't know what else could be done. I just had to keep going.

The problem was that each morning I set up my day with an intention to achieve what, in my opinion, was best for me. I would call upon God's promises only to try to get me closer to *my own agenda.*

If only I had done so with the intent to spend every moment in Him, with Him, for Him. Seeking Him with all of my heart. Surrendering to Him with trust and dwelling in His peace and provision. This isn't just my perspective or input—it's Scriptural and it's the Truth. It just took me about 28 years to start fully aligning myself with the Truth.

Before, I sought the blessings instead of the Blesser,

the gifts before the Giver,

the deliverance but not the Deliverer.

My day consisted of:

1. A lot of worship music.

2. Escaping out in nature despite being too severely malnourished and ill to be hiking for hours (I hadn't yet admitted to myself that I was literally depending on adrenaline and dopamine to get by, via exercise, and it was too much physically; mentally, I felt I had no other escape).

3. Buying a bunch of keto treats or making a bunch of keto treats—dopamine rush.

4. Spending too much money on massages or adjustments at the chiropractor. I also felt safe in those places. I felt somewhat understood. I needed safe places and safe people. I needed to be around people who looked at me and spoke to me like they really believed in me, and didn't just feel sorry for me, or even worse—doubted me or even looked down on me.

5. My day would end with a groaning. Not outward (not usually anyways), but inward. I felt so grateful for the nights that I would have no energy but to crash into bed. As awful as it sounds, I was so relieved to have that promise of being unconscious again—even if just for another few hours—to escape the pain.

I missed my family a lot. I thought of them every day, throughout the day. I thought of my dad, working on his computer, and wondered if he ever thought of me. I wondered if he was up to any new woodworking projects, or had learned new songs on the saxophone. I thought about my mom and her horse, and that she was probably enjoying having free comfortable range of her house again without me there.

I thought about my sister and niece. I wanted both of them to be proud of me. They didn't understand and they didn't make accusations one way or another. I prayed for them, because they were all going through a lot. Praying for others always felt so nice. It shifted my perspective. It also made me feel like I had value. Surely my prayers for others still meant something, even if I had felt totally abandoned.

NOW, I WAKE UP refreshed before the sun rises. I don't have pain in my body. I don't often feel grief or sorrow. I do not tolerate shame or fear—it is deliberately rejected with authority, and replaced with joy and confidence that comes from Christ alone. I often smile before I even open my eyes. I spend time alone with God before I do anything else, because this dictates how I face the day. My heart posture determines the outcome of the entire day. Grounding myself in God's Word is no longer just an intention. It's a non-negotiable. I don't want to live my life without Him. There is no true life without Him!

I voluntarily go to CrossFit six days per week.

I do not share this to brag in any way. I say this to point out that someone who used to get put on a time out during elementary school recess for becoming too flushed in the face, and someone who was once bedbound and could barely hold her own head up, is now doing all of these things on top of working full time and having the capacity to foster and give to relationships the way I've always *wanted* to. I have the capacity for which I have desired to live at my whole life. But not until very recently was I truly enabled and empowered to do so.

God has delivered, redeemed, and restored. I continue to feel better and better each day. I believe this has to do with upregulating hormones as well as continuous detox from oxalate—which can take up to ten years. My relationship with God continues to deepen and strengthen. He is the rock upon which I stand. It's only up from here.

And if I were ever to run into severe issues again, I would face them so differently. I don't fear that! There's nothing in this world and no one in this world that I fear. My hope is secure in the eternal and everlasting—where moths and rust do not destroy and where thieves cannot break and steal.

> *"Store your treasures in heaven, where moths and rust cannot destroy, and thieves do not break in and steal."*
>
> *—Matthew 6:20*

Healing didn't happen how I had imagined. It didn't happen at all until I released previous expectations that were outside of His provision and purpose.

The Lord heals wounds that are deeper than the ones we're usually asking for. Often, we are unaware of the areas in our lives that the Lord wants to restore.

He doesn't just want to see us free. He wants to captivate us. After everything I've gone through, and the way the Lord has carried me, I see that He is indeed *most high*. He is God, above it all. He does not settle. He doesn't allow us to make excuses because He knows that *He is enough*. I was too stubborn to surrender to His Grace until I had no other choice, but you don't have to be. He cannot lift you up until you yield and humble yourself before Him. That might be uncomfortable and challenging. You're very likely withholding areas in your life that He wants to change *if you're not challenged or uncomfortable*.God has changed me in ways that are so much greater than reversing autoimmune or Lyme disease, or even severe mood disorders.

God has freed me in a way that I can love selflessly. I can be vulnerable and put others before myself—even if it requires real sacrifice on my part—because of Jesus! I'm changed. My heart is no longer consumed with myself. I want to dwell in Him and He in me. I want to surrender to His will daily, because only then am I free of myself, and only then am I liberated from my flesh—by His Spirit.

This all might sound a bit heavy, but it's nothing new. Jesus Himself is the Way, the Truth, the Life. The Gospel, truly grasped, is life changing.

Faith is another key ingredient to freedom that I think is often misunderstood. Having faith isn't just a feeling. It's living like you believe. It means you're actively taking steps like what you have Faith for has already happened. It's having Faith *on* something, not just *in* something.

Charles Blondin became the first man to walk on a tightrope downstream from the Niagara Falls across the gorge in 1859. Blondin walked backward across the tightrope to Canada and returned pushing a wheelbarrow. I'm sure so much of the crowd cheered him on with confidence and admiration.

After pushing a wheelbarrow across while blindfolded, Blondin asked for participation from the audience. The one who was willing to get into that wheelbarrow would be the one with true Faith.

Are you just clapping for God or are you actually getting in the wheelbarrow? Because that's what it takes. He sees you, knows you, loves you, and wants all of you.

No matter where you're at right now or how hard it is, I promise you if you just hold on and keep choosing to have hope, one day you will live the life that you have prayed for and dreamt of. You are not the exception and you are not overlooked by God. But you do have to give yourself time and give yourself grace. You'll have to learn how to receive grace before you can give it, and that takes real strength and courage.

The Lord not only delivered me but he restored and blessed me beyond my wildest dreams. I see this all the time in my coaching—people actually surpass the goals or hopes they had started with. If things look bleak, it's still not fair to say that it will always be that way. Only God knows exactly what your neurotransmitters are doing or how your liver is going to function today. God knows all things and he will reveal to us the truth when we seek Him. He is the truth. He is life. He's above it all and he does care about the little things. It's the little things in life that make up a collection of most beautiful moments.

Healing is not linear. It has ups and downs. Things often look worse or *the worst* before they get better. Keep your eyes on what's above and ahead. Don't forget to embrace this present moment and the people in your life. Don't limit yourself, label yourself, or put yourself into any box.

"I praise you because I am fearfully and wonderfully made; your works are wonderful, I know that full well."

—Psalm 139:14 14

19

Nonlinear Healing

As much as I would like to look back and remember times that I was able to find comfort and peace in the midst of chaos, those moments were so few and far in between the long seasons of what felt like unending misery and mental, physical, spiritual, and emotional battle.

I went for nature walks to find solace and to be present, and to get out of my own head for just a moment, but I never did escape. Because wherever I went, there I was. Until I found total confidence and trust in the Lord, I would struggle with heavy fear and concerns of the future. I didn't have any peace. I was truly restless in my own striving.

Every day just felt like I was trying to make it to the end of the day. I had the same deep-rooted fear and anxiety no matter where I was or what I was doing. Each night I told myself "It's over. The worst must be over. It can't get any harder. Tomorrow will be better!". But it wasn't. It kept getting more difficult, stressful, chaotic, heartbreaking, and heavy. I was stuck in my own negative mental, physiological, and emotional state. I cried out to the Lord but also held him at an arm's length—I had become numb. I was hurting so much that I started to get rough edges. There wasn't any lightness in my life. Not around others, not alone. It was only sorrow and bitterness.

My routines kept me going. Things like brushing my teeth, keeping my room clean, and breathing in fresh air every day made me feel like I was still in the land of the living. It wasn't over yet. There is much danger to having too much time on our hands. And so when we are in a medically unstable state, we have to somehow find balance in not working and taking it easy. But what happens if we aren't recovering? What happens if we aren't moving forward? That's a dangerous place to be. Fear and discontentment reside in those places if we don't stand guard to keep them out.

It's good to work. We are created to be productive. We are created to thrive! We have gifts and talents that we are created to use to bring glory to God and to bless others with...

and when all that that falls to the wayside, we feel so awkward.

I did, anyway. I felt really awkward and uncomfortable.

Every day was a hard day.

Distractions hardly worked. My neurotransmitters were shot and my spirit was crushed.

It all changed when I surrendered. It felt so good to say "I give up! I'm not in control, anyway!" At least then, the pressure was off. I received grace and that grace lifted me up.

> "*He makes me as surefooted as a deer, enabling me to stand on mountain heights.*"
>
> —Psalm 18:33

Don't ask God to take away the struggle... Lean into adversity. Take responsibility in your *ability to respond*. Yes, it is scary. Let me assure you of this: It is uncomfortable to surrender all to Christ.

Ask God for his presence and his peace and his strength to get through it and even grow from it. Because with the right heart posture and attitude we can choose to let trials refine us and lead us into a deeper and more intimate relationship with Christ.

He takes failure, sorrow, disease, shame, fear and turns them for good. He did it for me and He will do it for you. I'm not any more special than any of you. God gave His only Son for you. He loves you. He will lift you up.

> "*Not only so, but we also glory in our sufferings, because we know that suffering produces perseverance; perseverance, character; and character hope.*"
>
> —Romans 5:3-5

These days, I really feel and experience that every day is a gift. I wake up refreshed and excited. I don't carry heaviness, not even for a moment. I walk in freedom and gratitude. I have joy deep in my spirit. I am not afraid. I am happy, I am healthy, and I am whole. I thank God and spend time with Him before I go to sleep. I wake up and start thanking Him before I do anything else.

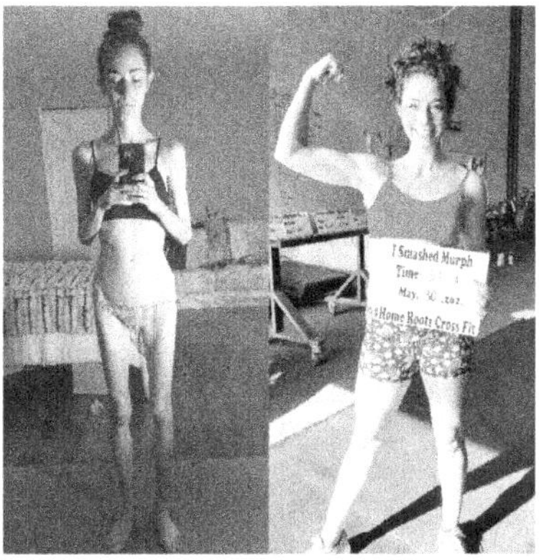

I am grateful for the ability to take a full breath, in and out. I won't forget the times that it was such a struggle to do even just that. I pray that I never do forget the severity of everything I've been through. Sometimes, we hold onto the good and forget the bad. And while I think that is mostly a good thing, I don't want to ever forget the sting of it all. The traumatizing events of my life have become pillars of hope for others, and a daily reminder that my God truly is the Healer, and that He really does love me!I am thankful for my strength and stamina. I do CrossFit now because it is a celebration of what my body can do!

I am thankful for my family and friends. I am thankful for the opportunity to help and love others.

One missing piece keeps an entire puzzle from being completed...

Perhaps you've hit a plateau or have been in a valley for long enough to start doubting if you're ever getting to where you want to be. Maybe you're doubting what you believe in or what you've been doing up until this point. Maybe you just doubt that there is a God who has a bright future in store for you. Maybe you're doubting yourself.

Doubt, when left to simmer, becomes toxic. The enemy wants you to be insecure, and an easier target to penetrate with his darts of discouragement. He is a master of deception who plays on our emotions. It is our responsibility to acknowledge and confront doubts, negative thoughts, and anything that sets itself up contrary to the Word of God—which is the only unchanging variable: The Truth.

> *"It is important for you to know that as a child of God, the enemy has absolutely no authority over you! In fact, in Jesus' name we have authority over all principalities of darkness."*
>
> —Luke 10:19

The enemy knows this, so his best bet is to trick you into forgetting your true identity as a child of God and the authority we have in Christ. He may also play on discouragement, bitterness, unforgiveness, grief, sorrow, fear, and shame. Sound familiar?

If you're feeling discouraged, please remember that God's grace is sufficient, for whatever season you are in. His Grace is enough for you to rise up in His strength above the circumstances.

> *"But you belong to God, my dear children. You have already won a victory over those people, because the Spirit who lives in you is greater than the spirit who lives in the world."*
>
> —John 4:4

He will turn what's ugly, difficult, and challenging into something for good, not only for you but for others. That's what He does. He *loves* to shine through broken vessels.

It can also be helpful to work with someone who can help you to troubleshoot and identify what that missing piece could be. Pray for discernment on who to work with. God provides in all sorts of ways, including bringing along those right people in due season. It's up to us to be receptive and open to what He is trying to lead us to.

It often gets darkest before the dawn, and things get worse before they get better.

Do not give up. There is always hope.

> *"Be sober-minded; be watchful. Your adversary the devil prowls around like a roaring lion, seeking someone to devour."*
>
> —Peter 5:8

> *"For our struggle is not against flesh and blood, but against the rulers, against the powers, against the world forces of this darkness, against the spiritual forces of wickedness in the heavenly places."*
>
> —Ephesians 6:12

> *"Look, I have given you authority over all the power of the enemy, and you can walk among snakes and scorpions and crush them. Nothing will injure you."*

—Luke 10:19

20

Fear Not

WHEN I WAS YOUNGER, there were so many things that I would read in the Bible that I could appreciate, but could not relate to.

One of these common subjects were talking and preaching about Christ. I grew up in a Christian home and was not ashamed to share that I was Christian, however I rarely felt led to share the good news or an overwhelming urge to share Jesus with others. I did have the Holy Spirit, who would prompt me to love others. He also reassured me in my times of darkness that I was not alone. Without that, I would have taken my own life on multiple occasions.

But these nudges were nothing like what I would read in Scriptures.

In May of 2019, when the Lord delivered me from near death and restored me to abundance greater than what I have ever known or prayed for, all of that changed.

The long journey and process of suffering from severe mood disorders, severe digestive issues, over 10 autoimmune diseases, chronic Lyme disease, chronic C. Diff, trauma in my childhood and into my young adult years, being near homeless, domestic abuse...

That provided the perspective and contrast that was needed for me to fully grasp the goodness of God and pressure—by desperation, to surrender to His grace. That's when the message of true hope became *real*.

I'm not saying that you should pray for bad things to happen...but I'm encouraging you to lean into adversity and trials, because God will turn it for good and you will become a light for others still in darkness. It's not about me, it's about what God has done through me.

For the first time in my life, I feel fully...me! My character has developed and I feel free to shine the way that God intended. I don't compare myself to others anymore and I don't strive to be approved by others. I am walking in freedom, confidence, and abundance in Christ.

It seems to me that a lot of people are lost in themselves. They lack a sense of belonging, or any calling on their lives. This world will offer us so many "highs" and "rushes", but nothing that lasts. Your soul is the price for these things. Self medication is a common behavior that I've observed—it can be with drugs, sex, alcohol, Netflix, Instagram, vaping... It's all the same in the way that it gives you a hit of dopamine and makes you feel good. But these things are empty—they have nothing of substance for our souls—and yet we invest so much of ourselves into habits and rituals that only draw us farther from God, and who we were created to be.

I belong to Jesus. I know who I am. I have confidence and joy that runs so rich and deep. His Love is greater and sweeter than any quick fix. I am striving—still—to immerse myself fully into His presence more than I do. To abide in Him and He in me. There can be nothing before Him. Most of us have made our own idols out of things that are not necessarily bad until they precede our relationship with Christ.

> "*But if I say I'll never mention the LORD or speak in his name, his word burns in my heart like a fire. It's like a fire in my bones! I am worn out trying to hold it in! I can't do it!*"
>
> —Jeremiah 20:9

We now have this light shining in our hearts, but we ourselves are like fragile clay jars containing this great treasure. This makes it clear that our great power is from God, not from ourselves.

We are pressed on every side by troubles, but we are not crushed. We are perplexed, but not driven to despair.

We are hunted down, but never abandoned by God. We get knocked down, but we are not destroyed.

Through suffering, our bodies continue to share in the death of Jesus so that the life of Jesus may also be seen in our bodies.

> "*But we continue to preach because we have the same kind of faith the psalmist had when he said, 'I believed in God, so I spoke.'*"
>
> —Corinthians 4:7-10 & 13

From May 2019 to May 2022, I went from the worst physically, mentally, emotionally, & spiritually to the best I've ever been physically, mentally, spiritually & emotionally. I only continue to feel stronger, more grateful, more joy, and surely free.

So again, as I wrap up with these last few chapters, what are the biggest takeaways?

Identify and remove (or more concisely—*surrender*) the interference. In my case, these were:

1. A need for control and narrow-minded thinking. I surrendered control (or the sense and strong desire for it) and *fully* surrendered to God's authority—before understanding what that would look like. This is still a daily thing: Entrusting my life into Him. God will ask you to do things that you don't want to do or even understand why he would ask you to do them. Trust Him! I promise what He has in store for you is greater than what you could ever even imagine. He loves you the most. He is your first Love.

2. Many of the so-called super foods such as turmeric, baby spinach, avocados—which for many can be very beneficial but for myself only exacerbated my 10+ autoimmune conditions, chronic Lyme disease, and the chronic C. Diff infection that almost depleted me to death. These are often included in "Keto" dishes because they are low carb! But some are also very high in toxic compounds.

3. Oxalates have been the greatest antinutrient to make an impact on me and tends to be the case with clients as well.

4. Many non-animal foods. Opt for animal foods—including the fats. Many plant fats contain salicylates which *can* be very irritating to the gut. Coconut oil, while being a saturated fat, still held me back in terms of healing my gut. Plant fats also do not contain the vitamins and other nutrients that animal fats do (I'm not against Keto. I am boldly emphasizing that animal-based is optimal).

5. I was removed from a toxic environment and the Lord provided a safe place for me to heal—through a complete stranger on Airbnb who truly had love in his heart. That stranger is Tyler Heishman, the man I love. The best things come in strange packages, including Airbnb's in the ghetto during a life crisis. It wasn't what I expected, but God *loves* to work that way, doesn't He? Life in Christ is an awesome adventure.

6. I removed negative and broken belief systems (replacing them with affirmations, renewing the mind with the Word). This takes time and consistency, and it will likely feel redundant and maybe even over-kill. It's not. God created us with neuroplasticity! It's an incredible thing that we can really unlearn, rethink, and uproot toxicity though "trees" and create new healthy ones. It takes intentionality and consistency. Learned behaviors die hard.

We must also provide a proper foundation to replace the interference with:

1. For myself, with only the most bioavailable, nutrient dense foods that God designed us to eat, digest, and assimilate—animal fat and animal protein. Humans are designed to digest meat. Cows and gorillas, with multiple stomach chambers, are designed to

digest and assimilate nutrients from plants.I also optimized which of these foods I was eating so as to avoid and *heal* histamine intolerance, balance omega 3:6 ratio, promote mitochondrial fusion, and systemic healing (which involves the CNS, immune system, and hormones). For me, this meant non-aged ruminant meats, mainly from Billy Doe Meats—a family-owned business located in Hoffman Estates, Illinois. Not only are they loving and kind, but they offer the highest quality, non-aged meat I've ever had! It is rare to source meat that has not been aged (even well-known grass fed companies will age beef for a minimum of thirty days). The Billy Doe Meats family met me in my crisis and they played a large role in my healing. They were the first company I asked to affiliate with when I kicked off my career as a full-time health and life coach. They have been a game changer for many of my clients.

2. True Faith—which has *nothing* to do with my own feelings and is only by God's Grace that *cannot be earned* and *is freely given* when I choose His way and surrender my own; it can't be both.

Obedience is an act of true Faith, not a requirement to earn salvation. A life transformed by Christ is one surrendered to Him, because there is nothing and no one better.

Faith is a precursor to the abundant life He promises.

Don't overcomplicate it with excessive testing, supplements, and therapies. You are fearfully and wonderfully made. Even if you're malfunctioning, you're not broken. And even if you're broken, you're not unfixable.

Step number one is recognizing and acknowledging the miracle that you actually are. Are you consciously aware of every breath you are taking as you read this? Probably not. That's just a miracle in itself.

You were created to thrive. I do not believe that God intended us to only do so with expensive supplements and most definitely not by overthinking, overanalyzing and worrying everyday. If you're regularly concerned and anxious about your health, that should be addressed!

"*Fear not*" is used 365 times in the Bible. God has got you covered and has reminded you for every moment of everyday to *trust him* and *fear not*.

Yet still, even firm believers sometimes take it only as a suggestion or an encouragement. In reality, this is a commandant. Worrying about something more than trusting God makes it an idol. That needs to be addressed and changed.

So, start there—at the root. Once you've gotten your priorities straight and are grounded, try praying about the next steps and using discernment from a place of peace instead of panic. Sometimes someone who has experience and knowledge can help you to implement necessary changes for your healing and growth.

But before you make any more decisions...

Fear not.

917

Afterword

In Closing...

For a while now, I have been stalling with the last edits of my book. I had been praying about what God wanted me to include because once it's published, I can't go back and change it. I don't see anything missing, but I really felt like I needed to wait.

Tyler proposed to me yesterday with his family here in town.

So Grateful

I've been able to spend the past few days with his family, and just in that, something in my heart has come alive again that I didn't know had faded into non-existence.

There is warmth and color where what before felt abandoned.

There is so much love and kindness and a sense of belonging.

God has restored all of the broken places—even the ones I forgot about. I couldn't be more grateful.

As I close out here, I would invite you to surrender everything to Jesus Christ. if you've ever wondered what that looks like, it's nothing complicated. It just has to be sincere and He will meet you where you are at and He will bless abundantly. His Word is a guide and He will speak through it, through others, and through His Spirit. It starts with a prayer, and it continues by making a choice every day to live for Him instead of yourself. It's leaving the past behind and pressing on to what is ahead.

If you carry guilt or shame, that is not from God and he does not want you to hold on to it. You can leave it for good at the cross, where it has been dealt with.

Remember that there is always hope and that you are fearfully and wonderfully made!

Timeline

Events from 2017 and onward

SUMMER 2017:
CHAPEL HILL EDU

FALL 2017:
MOVING BACK HOME

SPRING 2018:
C. DIFF DIAGNOSIS

EASTER 2018:
TRIP TO AUNT JUDY'S

SPRING 2019:
LIVING WITH BRIAN

SUMMER 2019
LIVING AT TYLER'S AIRBNB

MY TAILORED JOURNEY

FALL 2021:
FIRST TAILORED KETO HEALTH RETREAT

SPRING 2022:
SECOND TAILORED KETO HEALTH RETREAT

SUMMER 2022:
ENGAGED & MARRIED TO TYLER

Acknowledgments

Thank you

Thank you, Mom and Dad, for loving me the best you knew how. Thank you for teaching me to seek God first. Thank you for setting beautiful examples for me to follow.

Thank you, Laura and Emma, for inspiring me to be the best sister and Aunt you believed me to be. The times I felt most lost, I still felt known in that way. I love you forever and always.

Thank you, Dr Osborne and Dr Ronald Rebmann, for believing in me when most did not, and for cracking my back more times than I could ever count. You provided me physical and emotional relief. I am so grateful for you and your wonderful staff.

Thank you to my friends who either stuck close by my side, or checked in every so often. I am sorry for the times I was so aloof. I appreciate your kindness and love. Thank you for reminding me that this world still has a lot of love left in it—found in beautiful people.

Thank you to Danny and Maura Vega, Robert and Crystal Sikes, Shawn Baker, Brett Lloyd, Michelle Hurn, Hoda and the Billy Doe Meats family—you guys were pillars for me. Thank you for meeting me where I was at and showing me the same selfless love that Christ shows us all.

Thank you to all of the amazing companies I get to partner with! You guys do so much for this community, and I would surely find struggle without you! I am *so* grateful for you! Billy Doe Meats, Northstar Bison, Equip Foods, Redmond Real Salt and ReLyte, Carnivore Crisps and Carnivore Dog, Renue by Science (formerly Alive by Science), Aussie Trace Minerals...the list goes on!

Thank you to my friends across the world whom I've connected with via social media. You know who you are. You're probably the first ones to read this book! Thanks for joining me and for sharing your own healing journey. Please stay tuned and keep asking me for my cookbook. It's on the way! I hope to meet so many of you in person at my retreats and other gatherings.

Thank you to my clients—you give my life meaning and purpose. You inspire me the most. I pray for you, and I am so grateful for you. I am rooting for you. I am walking alongside you. I have so much love for you.

Thank you, Tyler, for all the things I couldn't ever put into words...

Thanks for believing in me before I believed in myself. Thanks for being true to yourself. Thank you for showing me that true love is sometimes tough and uncomfortable. Thank you for pushing me towards God. You've shown me love that I have prayed for and dreamt of my whole live. You're more than what I have prayed for. You're wonderful beyond words. You are a strong leader, with such a big and gentle heart. You inspire me so much. Thanks for making me yours. I love you!

Coaching With Me

Heal, Overcome, And Transform

I offer 1-on-1 health and life coaching as well as group and family coaching. I also offer in-home coaching (here in our home), and host health retreats every Spring and Fall—or for as long as the Lord provides.

This coaching not only involves nutrition. The goal is to help you understand what true freedom looks like in all aspects—with yourself, with food, with others, and in Christ.

My goal is to help you not only to heal at a systemic level, but also to gain the intuition and understanding that will guide you for the rest of your life so that you never have to pay anyone ever again.

I believe it's important to work from the bottom up and address matters at the root.

Simply get in touch to schedule your first session! Feel free to reach out with your questions or concerns as well.

Email me at rebekah@tailoredketo.health

Tailored Keto Health Retreats

Meet Your Tribe

It would be my joy to host you at the next Tailored Keto Health Retreat.

This experience is great for anyone is looking for healing, learning, rest, recovery, and a fresh perspective.

If community and fellowship is important to you, this time together is invaluable. You will leave with a tribe!

If you struggle to identify, diversify, or prioritize your nutrition goals and choices, this is another huge benefit of spending time together in person.

I will show you how easy, non-invasive, and convenient it is to eat optimally for your own bioindividual needs.

We are joined by special guests such as Sally Norton and Doctor Ken Berry, with many more to come!

I am always open to your suggestions or requests!

The location will vary with every retreat. There is bound to be one that suits your preference, whether you prefer sunshine & saltwater or mountains & trails.

Email me at rebekah@tailoredketo.health for more info on upcoming retreats!

S. PADRE ISLAND
ORIGINAL
EST 1836

Testimonials

Client Experiences

Giulia Bertola

This is me, Giulia Bertola! I was a very energetic girl. I played sports, I was always busy, and I ate everything! At some point in my life, I felt that something was wrong with my body. I was not well. I was always tired. As soon as I ate I was sick, panic attacks, pains all over my body. After many visits and doctors, I was diagnosed with fibromyalgia. But things have worsened since then. After work stress and two pregnancies, the situation had become more and more serious. I went from 80 kg to 49 kg, I had digestive pain, and I could no longer eat anything. I did a lot of research on nutrition because I just wanted to live!

Many types of food were recommended to me by non-competent people. They told me to do the Macrobiotic diet, and my situation degenerated. I was dying eating! I never gave up, and I started looking for a breakdown in nutrition. I started the Paleo diet, but it wasn't enough. I was still sick. I have not given up. I have searched again, studies, searches in English. I have translated many texts. I have been informed, and thanks to Instagram, I came across the carnivorous diet! I started this diet.

One evening, I found myself reading the story of Rebekah. It seemed similar to my story—so thin, but with a great strength to live! I decide to write to her and she replied immediately. From the beginning she gave me many tips with a written text so I could translate more easily! This is the way to heal my intestines! With her advice, I started eating fats and proteins to stabilize the levels of hypoglycaemia and my thinness. I ate in an 8 hour window and fasted for 16 hours. I cut out pork meat and ate organ meat, including liver! I decreased stress and took cold showers and hot saunas.

Rebekah has always been close to me and has quieted all my doubts. She gave me many tips on what to eat and how to cook fatty cuts. She recommended an integration to improve my intestinal problem and to get real salt and food! The bone broth she recommended is helping me a lot. It was really helpful to me. Now it's up to me to practice yoga and meditation to relax my muscles. Thanks to her help, so much Faith and hope in my recovery has come back, that God helps us! I know that my healing process will still be long, but I really think this is the right way after seeing so many improvements in my body.

Let's eat real food!

Christina Barron

I am 47 years old and have suffered from hormonal problems and many autoimmune-like issues for several years. I also have severe allergies and hypothyroidism. I've been to several traditional doctors and functional doctors, and I've worked with different health coaches over the last 15 years just to be left with nothing but empty pockets and frustration. I have spent hundreds of dollars on supplements as well. Nothing helped. I ended up with more issues.

I have experimented with every diet you can think of in search of health. I found the most success with keto and fasting. I lived that lifestyle for two years and eventually transitioned to a carnivore way of eating for 14 months to squash any lingering health problems. While I had success on my own, I felt I was at the point where I was regressing. I was getting constant hives and having cycle issues. I was feeling incredibly lost and fearful because of my symptoms.

I came across Rebekah's story on a podcast and found so many similarities between us. I honestly thought that she could help me get to a healthy place again. I'm happy I decided to work with her. Rebekah has been God sent. She coached me for six months and through many complicated situations. She remained steadfast. She never gave up on me, even when I felt like I had no hope of being well again. Rebekah offered me clear recommendations, and she always listened to how I felt.

Rebekah has been a massive part of my support system. While I'm still on my healing journey, several issues have been resolved for me. I have been able to lower my thyroid medication, improve my sleep and stress levels, regulate my cycle, expand my diet without an allergic reaction, and improve my body composition tremendously. She also guided me through fasting appropriately for my situation. Most importantly, she helped me lose my fear and find my Faith again. I'm no longer living with a fear-based mentality. I now have the tools along with every bit of confidence, knowing that I'm on the right track to continue healing.

Thank you from the bottom of my heart, Rebekah!

Alexandria Rossi

I created an Instagram account on a random summer day in 2020 to find support after being diagnosed with narcolepsy—a neurological condition that often makes someone extremely exhausted. It's debilitating, to say the least. Minutes after getting my account, I found Rebekah's page after searching for #narcolepsy. She also supported the ketogenic diet, something I'd found some success with in the past in my binge eating recovery. I also suffer from clonazepam withdrawals, something Rebekah had toiled with, too. I'd never met anyone who had struggled with narcolepsy and benzo withdrawals, and also ate like me. And seeing how Rebekah used food and her Faith to heal herself from countless autoimmune diseases, I wanted to work with her. And now I have a friend for life.

She counseled me for three months and was the best nutritionist I have ever had. And I've had quite a few nutritionists and dietitians after battling several eating disorders— namely binge eating (food addiction, honestly). I sought to lose 25 lbs in three months. I didn't lose the weight. I lost some, but I lost what was more important. I lost less focus on other people, meaning I cut down self-comparisons big time. I lost some of my grip on my expected timeline for reaching my goals. I didn't lose this all by myself. It's because God put Rebekah on my path, and Rebekah graciously rose to the challenge of helping me whenever I needed help.

I loved how Rebekah didn't push a diet on me. She is all about what works best for a person, and that may need to be discovered through trying different things. She believed my story and why I had the various food hang-ups I had due to major obsessive-compulsive disorder (OCD) and PTSD. She encouraged me when I was used to beating myself up. Basically, she taught me to be my own best friend. Rebekah helped me conquer the biggest obstacle: my fear of losing weight. I'd been ridiculed in the past for losing weight. She helped me understand that God wants me to live a vibrant life.

Rebekah helped me understand that a challenge—even suffering, yes—can be beautiful, if we choose our mindset. For me, suffering was not giving into OCD patterns or to criticism from others about how I eat. I also have PCOS and endometriosis and cannot "eat normally," in the Standard American diet-sense. Not everyone welcomes a carb-less plate.

Lastly, money doesn't have to be a barrier to better health. Rebekah will work with you regarding an extremely reasonable payment plan, as she has for me. Rebekah does this work because she truly loves to serve others. I hardly write testimonials for stuff. But I want others to be blessed with the experience and growth I have had. Wouldn't you want a nutritionist and coach who helps you lose—and gain—what you truly need?

Polina S.

I would really like to share all the improvements that I've experienced so far. I was diagnosed with clinical depression and panic/anxiety attacks 7 years ago. I had these horrible attacks 24/7, and I am not joking. For some people, they might last for hours, but my nervous system was completely shut down. I couldn't sleep, eat, or move. Antidepressants helped to ease the symptoms, but I would still wake up every morning with my arms shaking. It took me hours to open my eyes because I was so afraid to go through that hell every morning again, and again, and again.

Now, for the first time, I wake up at 9 am (not at 12 or 1 pm) with no signs of panic attacks and feel the energy to get up from the bed and start a new day. 1.5 years ago, I was bedbound with excruciating pain all over my body (including face and jaw muscles). I did a lot to reduce this pain on my own, but the pain wouldn't go away completely. Especially my legs hurt, so it was very painful to walk, not to mention how I missed dancing to my favorite music. Yesterday I was dancing in the kitchen for the first time.

Pain is still present. It is not a quick process, but it's slowly, gradually going away. I notice I am becoming physically capable of doing more things (after years of weakness). Based on my arm tracker, I hadn't had a deep sleep phase for almost 2 years. It was always either 15-20 minutes or nothing at all. I was constantly tired and didn't recover properly through the night. I had severe insomnia for years and sometimes would lie in bed, eyes open till morning. Now I finally have my decent 1 hour 24 minutes of deep sleep phase and I can feel I sleep well, even though I am still adapting.

I also had skin issues. Not severe, but it was constantly inflamed, and it usually took a lot of time to cover my face with concealer before going out with family and friends. I do not use it anymore. A few days ago I did my blood test and noticed that my lymphocytes went down. I had chronic inflammation (high lymphocytes/low neutrophils) for years. Extremely weak immune system, herpes flare-ups once or twice per month. Lymphocytes would go up to 47-52% (with a normal range from 19 to 37%) and neutrophils were ~38% (normal range from 45 to 70). Now my lymphocytes are 43% and neutrophils are 44. There is definitely an improvement! Erythrocytes and hematocrit came back to normal. No more red marks and, except for lymphocytes and neutrophils, my blood test is excellent.

I was surprised how comfortably my period started this month. For many years, I had horrible premenstrual syndrome. The first few days were so painful and difficult I would lie in bed for hours, taking painkillers. If I hadn't known when to expect my period, I would never have believed I was going through the premenstrual phase almost symptom-free.

Allergic reactions—gone. Skin allergies—gone. Depression is gradually disappearing, as if a huge black cloud over my head is melting away. My arms and legs are no longer cold like ice. I have noticed improvement in my vision. My fingernails grow stronger and I no longer lose a significant amount of hair when I brush it (thought I would become bald one day, hah).

I am officially a month into carnivore after my consultation with Rebekah. There is a lot of work to do and a huge healing journey ahead of me. But now I know that there is something worth fighting for. And really want others to believe there is always hope. Even if it feels like you've lost it so many times along the way.

Jennifer Geissert

Mid Vacation Update: I'm feeling so great, I just wanted to share!

My skin continues to heal. I'm excited to wake up every morning and notice the subtle improvements. But I've noticed some even more powerful changes on this vacation. In the past, I've struggled so much with binge eating. I've never been on a vacation (especially one with free food and drinks everywhere) and not come home having gained at least 10 lbs and a ton of inflammation. This time, I feel like freaking Wonder Woman. I feel confident and proud of my body even when walking around in a bikini. I haven't weighed myself, but my body is not fluctuating or getting more and more bloated or puffy as each day passes. I realize some might find this revelation a little superficial, but it's a very serious topic for me.

In the past, I would gain a bunch of weight, as I mentioned, but the really troublesome weight was mental. I would feel fairly good about myself on the first day of vacation and become progressively more miserable as each vacation day passed. I ended up feeling completely out of control around food, like a failure, like I wanted to hide my body, and embarrassed when I returned home and didn't fit into my clothes anymore. That mental weight was very heavy and probably bordering on mild depression. Even worse, it took weeks or months to get back on track after returning home. It was a never-ending cycle.

I honestly don't feel like I've even had to employ much discipline on this vacation in order to stick to my carnivore diet. There are yummy looking sweets and drinks everywhere, but that magnetic pull doesn't seem to be there anymore. I think there are two reasons why.

1.) I feel so good about my body, and for the first time ever, that feeling isn't accompanied by a fear of losing all my progress and feeling like a failure.

2.) I'm not experiencing insatiable cravings. I guess when you fuel your body with nutrient-dense foods, like fat and protein, it doesn't desire all the carbs and chemicals and dopamine increasing sugars. I knew those things to be true before, but I never experienced them myself. Now I get it!

My typical diet here had been steaks, salmon (sometimes cooked, sometimes raw), shrimp, and my favorite: the meat from ribeye tacos. It's so fatty and delicious! If hungry, I supplement with beef jerky and beef sticks I brought from home. And I've been drinking plain water or soda water with a lime. The soda water keeps me from feeling "left out" when others are enjoying all the free drinks.

It's amazing how this "restricted" diet has allowed me to feel more FREE than ever during my vacation. I'm so proud of myself, so excited about what's to come, and so happy to share it with you.

Christina Maiorano

Hello! My name is Christina Maiorano and I'm extremely honored to have worked with Rebekah. Rebekah is a caring, compassionate, and knowledgeable health and wellness coach. Her expertise and experience in overcoming her own health issues has been an integral part of my journey to gut healing. In 2018, I was diagnosed with SIBO. Having SIBO brought about digestive issues and many food sensitivities, including histamine issues. With this, I began researching how to heal the gut.

I worked with a nutritionist, a functional medicine doctor, and a GI doctor. It literally took a village to rid me of SIBO! In 2019, after testing negative for SIBO, I still needed much support to heal and continued to pursue my research. I came across the Carnivore Diet and began reading how this diet has had a positive effect on healing digestive issues. Shortly after, I discovered and joined the Women Carnivore Tribe on Facebook where I met Rebekah!

I worked with Rebekah for the last 3 months. Within this short time, she has helped me in more ways than I could have possibly expected! Rebekah is a kind, caring, and non-judgemental young lady. There is a calmness about her that helps people overcome their insecurities. She is always ready to offer positive suggestions on how to improve your lifestyle. For me, she was the support I needed to help me recognize the strong woman I am and how much I have accomplished on my journey to heal and be healthy again. She also taught me how to be kind to myself and give myself grace when life is not so perfect.

To me, Rebekah is not just a health and wellness coach. She is a *true friend*. If you are looking to *change* your lifestyle, *heal* your health issues, and *improve* your wellbeing, I encourage you to reach out to Rebekah!

Shely M.

I've been working with Rebekah for a year to overcome my autoimmune disease. My diagnosis is Diffuse Systemic Sclerosis (Scleroderma). It's one of the most dreadful autoimmune issues. Many doctors say it's worse than Lupus. I found out that I have an autoimmune disease since January 2021, while maybe from a long time ago symptoms have been progressing slowly without me realizing it. I have written a testimony before (after being 2 months carnivore), this is my update testimony after I have been carnivore for a year. I don't know how to make this story short, but I can start by telling you this: *Rebekah has helped me a lot*!

She is exactly how a coach should be: a motivator and a mentor, in her unique way, which worked for me! In summary, there are three top things that I learned from Rebekah:

1.) How to practically strengthen Faith and correct mindset facing a chronic disease (or adversity in general).

2.) How to build intuition about our body, read symptoms, and do simple steps continuously and consistently to overcome it. These steps usually include a carnivore diet, other natural modalities like breathing exercises, stretching exercises, infrared therapy, and so forth. Sometimes supplements are needed, but very few types.

3.) How to stay calm during flare ups or stressful times, wait on God's cues (in this case it is usually readable from the body's symptoms), pick yourself up, and build courage to continue your journey.

Although we have different religion, Rebekah and I both believe in God and from there we gained strength to make things work. The first months were not easy. There were days when I was so panicked during a flare-up. But Rebekah calmed me down. She shook my anxiety like a leaf and kept telling me, "You got this. God does not leave you. He loves you and is with you every step of the way." So then I ate some fat, read some Qur'an verses, heated myself with my infrared lamp, and finally was able to sleep.

Rebekah also has this practical mind that I adore, because I tend to overcomplicate things. She could see through or had experience with a list of overlapping symptoms that I told her about, draw a conclusion from them, and then make 1-2 steps of recommendation. I found this was easier to apply to my sensitive body system. I once read her client referred to this skill as 'finding the nugget'. I couldn't agree more! This way is a lot more effective than taking a bunch of medications or supplements, which often were too much and made my body clog up or flare up in the end.

After a year on the carnivore diet under Rebekah's guidance, I have gained tremendous progress, especially in energy, weight gain, and stable mood. From a year ago, not being able to stand in a proper shower due to Raynauds and my weak condition where I couldn't lift my hands for too long, to today, being able to do yoga classes with 'normal and healthy' people. I gained mostly healthy weight from 42 kg (92.6 lbs) to 48 kg (106 lbs), with my height of 157 cm (5 ft 1.8 in) I have reached my ideal bodyweight within a year. I can also use my brain again for working. I'm an architect, by the way. My energy level is enough to go up and down other people's stairs to be involved in their house renovation.

Until today, I can't believe from mostly the meat diet I can gain this much life again. I honestly thought I was going to be in a wheelchair from last year! Although I still have some stubborn symptoms that need to be resolved, my intuition, knowledge, and calmness have developed so much that I can now make better decisions about what to do. I consulted with doctors and could extract information from them, choose only the recommendations that I needed, taking two tests instead of five. Being able to make decisions about my own body is so empowering!

I consulted with Rebekah whenever I needed her to help me find the nugget among so much new information I received from doctors or anything I read online. She's aware of my sensitive system, so I know she's going to make a careful and selective suggestion. Within an hour of consultation, we came up with a plan that hopefully can combat the remaining stubborn symptoms.

Thank you all for reading my story. If you need to ask more about it, you can find me at Instagram @itsmeshely. I hope this comes as an inspiration for your own faith and health journey.

Abbey Jackson

Rebekah has truly saved me from what I was becoming.

For about a year, I did great with counting calories and maintaining my macronutrient counts every day. I lost 70 lbs on my own. In April 2019, I took on a full-time job, and no longer had the time to meal prep and count my calories every day. I was extremely stressed. I began binge eating every single day, lost my drive in the gym, and struggled worse than I ever had with my mental health. I have been dealing with depression and anxiety since I was 12 years old.

I started working with Rebekah on January 15, 2020, and my life has changed dramatically. I'm living a life that I've never experienced before. I feel free from my addiction to food. My mental health is the best it has been in years and I feel as though I'm finally able to appreciate things in my life that I wasn't able to before. She taught me how to cook foods so that my options weren't limited, went shopping with me, and showed me that I can eat without counting calories and still be successful. She also taught me about how Ketosis works, so I would further understand why it isn't necessary to track. I am no longer miserable and trapped within myself. I have the energy to get through each day. I can focus on the tasks I am working on, and I finally feel like I'm getting my life under control at 20 years old. I chose not to take care of myself for years and this is the first time I have invested in myself in a long time and I never knew how dramatic the difference could be.

Not only am I grateful for this journey and Rebekah, but my friends, family, and boyfriend are as well. They have all seen me at my worst and now they are seeing me on my way to being my best. I can't wait to see how much more I can improve. Not to mention that I've already lost roughly 18 lbs since my last doctor's appointment on December 28, 2019. These are massive accomplishments for me, and I'll forever be grateful for what Rebekah has done for me.

Janine

I could have never committed to this diet or developed any confidence in this way of eating if it weren't for Rebekah. For context, I have had severe RA in nearly all joints for over 17 years, along with several other health issues (chronic hives, acne, interstitial cystitis, anxiety, yeast infections, and so on). When I first tried to go carnivore on my own, I actually ended up in a terrible place—a severe UTI and awful joint pain.

Rebekah helped me connect all the pieces I was missing. She taught me the importance of ketosis and helped me immensely through the keto flu with emotional support and electrolyte information. And then we troubleshooted various issues (e.g. chronic yeast infections) for 9 months together.

My healing journey has NOT been linear, and Rebekah always warned me of this. But I do feel my body getting stronger (I'm actually now lifting weights and working with a trainer, whereas I couldn't do this before), my sleep is getting better, my skin is less itchy, and I have healed from a lot of food intolerance. The joints go through periods of good and bad still, but I am exercising patience as I know I have more healing to do.

Throughout this process, Rebekah has always been honest and committed. She's talked me off the ledge of panic attacks, identified patterns where I was sabotaging progress (hello late nights out with alcohol), and was readily available when I needed a quick response.

I consider her a friend and an inspiration. I feel exponentially more confident experimenting on my own now after working with her, and feel a sense of safety knowing I can go back to her when needed.

For anyone in need of guidance and support, Rebekah is here for you. I cannot thank her enough.

HAPPY
HOUR

Discounts

Vitality Is Invaluable, But Discounts Help!

Brands that I stand by!

Billy Doe Meats

"TAILORED" for 10% off the Best low histamine, Halal Lamb, Goat & Veal

Northstar Bison

"TAILORED" for 10% off Northstar Bison!

Equip Foods

15% off Equip Protein Powder!

Aussie Trace Minerals

"TAILORED10" for 10% off Aussie Trace Minerals

Redmond Real Salt

"Tailored" for 10% off Redmond Real Salt

Miracle Noodles

"Tailored" for 10% off Miracle Noodles!

Perfect Keto

"Tailored" for 10% off Perfect Keto ketovore-goodies

Fora

"Tailored" for 10% off my fav glucose & ketone monitor!

Grassland Nutrition

"tailored10" for 10% off Grassland Nutrition Products (Low histamine, freeze-dried organs & suet)

Carnivore Crisps

"TAILOREDKETO" for 10% off Carnivore Crisps!

Renue By Science

"tailoredketohealth10" for 10% off Renue By Science products - NMN, NAD & more - NOOTROPICS are rad!

Best Bone Broth

"TAILORED" for 10% off Best Bone Broth Concentrate for Reduced Histamine

The Carnivore Bar

The Carnivore Bar!! "TAILORED" at checkout for 5% off

Keto Rubs

"tailored15" for 15% off Keto Rubs!

Osso Good Life

"TAILORED" for $10 Osso Good Co. Bone Broth!! (CLEAN, low oxalate, deep flavor- perfect for on the go!)

Just Thrive Health

Use "rebekah10″ for 10% off Just Thrive Probiotics (the only probiotic I trust!)

Arboleaf

"Tailored" for 20% off Arboleaf Massage Gun

KOZE Red Light

"Tailored" for 10% off KOZE Red Light Therapy

Jigsaw Health

"tailoredketo10″ at checkout for $10 off Jigsaw Health Products!

Santa Cruz

"Tailored" for 15% off Santa Cruz Medicinals CBD

Happee Dawg

"TAILOREDKETO" FOR 10% OFF Happee Dawg real food and primal treats

Infinite Age Co

Use code "tailoredketo10″ for 10% off Infinite Age products!

Bioptimizers

TAILOREDKETO10 for 10% off BiOptimizers

Mind Bullet

"KETOHEALTH" for 20% off Mind Bullet Kratom (Do your research or ask me about it first!)

Beauty By Earth

"TAILOREDKETOHEALTH12"

Jakab Bluelight Blockers

Code "Tailored" for 10% off Bluelight Blocking Glasses & Red Light Therapy

Purity Coffee

Code "Tailored" for 10% off Purity Coffee

Visit my website https://tailoredketo.health/ to see the most up-to-date version of my discount list!

About Author

Rebekah Heishman, Tailored Keto Health

Rebekah Heishman is a health & life coach with a keen eye for maximizing every diet's nutritional value. Ever since she was young, she has always had a passion for health, nature, fitness, and holistic medicine. She has overcome over 10+ autoimmune illnesses along with osteoporosis, costochondritis, and degenerative disc (which she was diagnosed with in 6th and 7th grade), OCD, anxiety, depression, insomnia, Narcolepsy, chronic Lyme disease, chronic C. Diff, and a myriad of digestive issues such as gastroparesis, IBS, IBD, slow transit colon, Celiac, and diverticulitis. She overcame all of it in the span of only a few years, and found total health and food freedom through Faith and proper nutrition. She has since directed her practice toward walking alongside others who are on their own healing journeys, helping them find optimal health through supporting their bioindividual needs.

Instagram:

https://www.instagram.com/tailoredketohealth/

Facebook:

https://m.facebook.com/TailoredKetoHealth

YouTube:

https://www.youtube.com/@rebekahheishman-tailoredke8939

Mail:

rebekah@tailoredketo.health

Tailored Keto Health Website:

https://www.tailoredketo.health/

TAILORED KETO HEALTH

SUSTAINABLE HEALTH ~ LABEL FREE ~ HEALING

Printed in Dunstable, United Kingdom

65010849R00129